More than Metaphors

Strategies for Teaching Process Writing

Stephen K. Smuin

⚛ Addison-Wesley Publishing Company

*Menlo Park, California • Reading, Massachusetts • New York
Don Mills, Ontario • Wokingham, England • Amsterdam • Bonn • Sydney
Singapore • Tokyo • Madrid • San Juan • Paris • Seoul, Korea • Milan
Mexico City • Taipei, Taiwan*

This book is published by the Alternative Publishing Group.

Managing Editor: Diane Silver
Editors: Bernard Brodsky and Micki Zatz
Production Coordinator: Karen Edmonds
Design and Production: Michelle Taverniti

ISBN 0-201-45501-3

1 2 3 4 5 6 7 8 9 10-AL-96 95 94 93 92

To Keely,
whose caring and support made it safe
to take the personal and professional
risks needed to complete this book

• *A First Word* •

No person creates in a vacuum, especially a teacher. In developing this book I have drawn from a plethora of areas for ideas, including the world of sports, ballet, literature, television commercials, newspaper stories, everyday life experiences, and from those serendipitous moments in bed late at night or early in the morning in the shower. I have observed a multitude of master teachers (both old and young) in a variety of disciplines and school settings. I have borrowed and traded activities with teachers and authors; I have modified and adapted strategies suggested by others so that they would fit the focus of this book. Exercises have been sent to me; lessons have been taken from teacher methodology textbooks; and some writing activities have made the rounds so thoroughly that no amount of research could determine their original sources. While I take full responsibility for all that is contained here, special thanks go to those authors whose books are quoted directly in my text. But the primary source for this book is my 20 years of classroom teaching, working with students and teachers from second grade through graduate school.

Creating a book is not merely a writing process—it is a living and learning process. Your professional experiences and environment help create your final product. Thus I am indebted to my colleagues at Nueva Learning Center, particularly Dr. Anabel Jensen and my Middle School staff.

But more importantly, this book is a result of my students, especially those at Nueva, who have taught me to be a better writing teacher and a better person—this book is really yours.

And finally, thanks, too, to the many other people who contributed directly and indirectly to this book; though your names are not listed, your efforts have not been forgotten.

—Stephen K. Smuin
Seeley Lake, MT
July 31, 1991

• Contents •

UNIT 4. CREATIVELY AMBIGUOUS WRITING ASSIGNMENTS   108

UNIT 5: PUTTING IT ALL TOGETHER: MAJOR PAPERS   120

Appendix   186

Bibliography   192

• *Preface* •

About Writing and This Writing Book

Writing is hard work. We learn to write primarily by writing, not by reading, studying literature, or memorizing parts of speech. Writing is a process, as is thinking. Merely assigning written work is not teaching students how to write.

This book attempts to bring some creativity, joy, and precision to the teaching of writing—a process which at times can be most frustrating to even the most accomplished writer. It is designed to teach you how to teach your students to write. Thus the developmental format of this book begins with a discussion on the nature of writing and the communication process; it then proceeds from introducing words, phrases, and sentences to the development of paragraphs, essays, and major papers.

The major goal of this book is to present strategies for teachers to utilize with students who want to write, but cannot get beyond staring at a blank sheet of paper. A blank page does not indicate a blank mind but a student who has not been taught how to write; every student has a lot to write about.

The strategies and activities in this book have been used with students ranging from the nonwriting fifth grader to the advanced adult writer. Because this book is intended to teach the process of developing a written piece of work, the strategies can be adapted for any stage of a student's intellectual or skill development.

It is my firm belief than any competent teacher can open this book to page one on the first day of class and begin teaching writing, proceed to the last day of class with the final activity and have each student be a significantly improved writer. However, the book also lends itself to teachers who wish to determine where their class is in learning the writing process and then pick and choose which sections to use.

This book is a resource, a tool. The single most important ingredient of an exciting, creative, stimulating classroom is you, the teacher. What you bring to these strategies, how you adapt them to your curriculum, how you expand them is what will determine the measure of success of your writing program. Every one of my students who has gone through the writing program outlined in this book has become a more enthusiastic, stimulated writer.

How to Use This Book

This is not primarily a book of writing assignments. How to teach writing, not how to assign writing, is the primary goal of this book. You will be asked to present material orally and then elicit responses from the students. You will determine when you've given enough examples and students are ready to move from "oral writing" to in-class writing. You must decide when they have shared enough in-class writing and are ready for homework. It is you, not the book, that must decide if the class should do several assignments on one technique.

This is a unique writing book in the sense that it is a book to be read by the teacher; it is not designed simply as a workbook for students. Much of teaching the writing process will be done orally. Most of the book follows a consistent process. It is unusual because it de-emphasizes the quantity of writing students need to do and emphasizes well-written shorter assignments focused on a specific skill:

1. The teacher makes an oral presentation to class: raising a question, teaching a skill, identifying a process, (or whatever).

2. The teacher has students demonstrate their understanding of the concept by offering "oral writing examples," or the teacher demonstrates written work on board (modeling).

3. Students demonstrate their working knowledge of the concept by writing in class and then sharing with class for feedback from teacher and peers.

4. Students are assigned written assignments that further strengthen their ability to utilize this new skill or concept; this can be done in class or as homework.

5. During the next class period the teacher passes back previous papers and gives students comments on common errors, misunderstandings, or areas of expertise and growth.

6. The new assignments due that class period are shared orally and then collected by the teacher; the teacher then begins a new presentation.

How much time to devote to each of these steps is up to you. You need to constantly take your class's writing temperature. How much oral practice do they need? How much sharing works best for them? How much peer editing should you do? How much time should you set aside for conferencing with students individually while students write in class?

There are a multitude of approaches for each of the strategies in this book. The value of this book is that it provides a framework and a strong philosophical base. You can decide where to begin with this book. Because of the logical organization, you can determine where your class should start, how much time should be spent on a skill or technique, and when to move on to new material. Where one activity is dependent upon another it is clearly indicated. The first unit, "On Writing," is a practical and philosophical discussion about writing. It is designed to provide you and your class a framework for all that will be taught and written .

The following unit, "Introducing Writing to Your Class," presents the basic concepts of writing to your class. These strategies are designed to intrigue and challenge reluctant writers as well as provide new vistas for those students already immersed in the writing process.

"Developing the Tools of the Writer," the third unit, begins to explore the three-phase process of writing: prewriting, writing, and revision. A multitude of activities are presented to introduce and master these three vital steps of writing.

"Creatively Ambiguous Writing Assignments," the fourth unit, provides writing assignments which are not just clever topics, but have a writing goal in mind. Each of the assignments demands that students bring thinking, creativity, and problem solving to the writing process.

The final unit, "Putting It All Together," covers major writing projects for students who have become competent with the skills and process of writing.

1. On Writing

*T*his unit is extremely important to understanding the philosophical basis for this book. Since the book is about learning how to teach writing, it is important that you be well grounded in the philosophical nature of teaching this craft. These four chapters should provide all the necessary background material for structuring a new writing environment in your classroom. It will discuss the why's, as well as explain the how's.

• *Writing as a Tool of Language* •

Clear writing indicates clear thinking. An original idea poorly communicated is a lost idea. As *New York Times* columnist William Safire states, "The way you write reflects the way you think, and the way you think is the mark of the kind of person you are."

Any successful writing program teaches writing and thinking as two interrelated processes. Some teachers are reluctant to tell students that their writing lacks clarity, is too verbose, or is devoid of specifics for fear it would make students reluctant to write again. It is true that editing and evaluating students' work must be done with great sensitivity and intelligence, but it must be done. An entire section in this book is devoted to techniques on how to accomplish that task.

Writing is a communication process—the most difficult one. When engaged in conversation with someone, the responsibility for communication rests on both people. You talk, I listen. If I don't understand, I ask questions. You clarify, give examples, restate. I indicate understanding; then we move to the next point. Dialogue. But written communication is a one-way process. The responsibility for communication is totally the writer's. Incoherent prose is like a television set turned on in an empty room: lots of transmission, but no reception.

A young child who sits down at the piano for the first time can play notes, but these do not create music. Music is organized notes; writing should be organized words.

Thus writing and thinking must go hand in hand; the teacher's role in a writing class—any class—is to teach that process. Writing is the physical expression of what you think. As one student put it, "How do I know what I think until I've put it in writing?"

• Ambiguity as a Tool in Teaching Writing •

Sometimes, writing is used as an evaluation tool rather than as a teaching tool. We evaluate students through their writing without ever having taught them to write. Writing as a teaching tool needs to take its rightful place next to discussion, inquiry, simulation, and lecturing. Students must write in all disciplines and use all disciplines to write.

One way of integrating thinking and writing is in the kinds of assignments that are given to students. Bob Samples writing in *Learning* magazine (April–May, 1984) asks, "Are your assignments clear and precise?" and then adds, "Too bad." The process of education is figuring out what to do when you don't know what to do, and Samples feels that assignments with carefully designed ambiguity resulted in students becoming "excited, effective, creative learners when given permission to explore and discover in ways not predetermined by overly prescriptive, highly specific assignments." The point is not, however, and Samples would surely agree, to tell the class, "You have a term paper due at the end of the semester and it can be on any subject you are really really interested in, and the length should be long enough to cover the subject." This is not creative ambiguity but lack of focus or purpose. Ambiguity with specificity is the desire.

The assignments in this book contain planned ambiguity. The goal is not to create ambiguous responses but to allow for a full range of responses. There is not *the* right answer. When students are asked to describe the sound thinking makes, you are not only working on the technique of description, but integrating problem solving, decision making, and thinking into the writing. The process is much more involved than asking a child to describe a favorite toy or day at the beach.

The likely response to many of the assignments in this book may be, "I don't know what to do." As an immediate reaction that is fine. It indicates the students will have to do some serious thinking before they do know what to do. Writing an essay to explain time or to analyze the functioning of a machine they have just invented creates ambiguity in what to write about, but more importantly it allows for the student to own that writing. The writing becomes important to them. *Learning* magazine's Judy Morris explains, "When the children write, it doesn't matter what they write about . . . what is crucial is that what they write be important to them." Ambiguous assignments can help stimulate important new relationships, while at the same time structuring the skill or technique on which you want students to work. This planned ambiguity is much different than saying "write an essay on any topic you wish."

A goal of this book is for you to develop your own creatively ambiguous assignments. Here is how this process works. Suppose that the goal of your lesson is to work on writing directions. Students are to learn the necessity for clear, precise statements. Many teachers have had students write directions on how to tie a shoe and then watch the class disrupt in laughter as students attempt to follow these "directions" to tie a shoe. But an assignment could also fulfill the goal of introducing direction writing with an assignment that asks students to give directions on how to create rainbows, how to color the clouds, how you can catch a Gzermp at night. Students can move on to writing the directions from school to their house, how to run the new computer software program, how to tune the carburetor, how to change a tire, how to turn off the gas in the house, how to get a date to the prom, how to make a friend, how to depollute the earth, or whatever.

The assignment on creating rainbows is the prewriting activity designed to introduce the skill of direction writing in a creative, yet ambiguous way; does anyone know *the* way to construct a rainbow? It provides a step towards moving to more concrete examples of the skill. It forces students to think, to be creative while working on a necessary skill of writing: precision in giving directions.

Once the creative assignment has been given, the teacher should then concentrate on teaching the skills necessary to complete the assignment, not in giving suggestions for how to do the assignment.

Are those students who, when faced with the television being turned off, respond, "Now what do I do?" the same ones who were fed overly prescriptive, non-deviating directions for essays that required no thinking, just plugging into the teacher's usual formula?

• *Writing as a Process* •

The three primary goals of writing should be *clarity, brevity,* and *specificity.* Students need to focus their writing to meet these three goals. The activities contained in this book are all developed with the idea of teaching students to write clear, brief, specific prose. From the first day of class until students get their diploma, they should be continually reminded of these goals, and their work evaluated in terms of these criteria.

The three-step writing process students use to create clear, brief, specific prose is: *prewriting, writing, revision.*

Generally it is the first and last steps that are sometimes neglected by teachers. They tell students to do it, expect students to do it, but never teach them *how* to do it. Students put pen to paper prematurely. A germination period is needed where a student is allowed to think, doodle, outline, cluster, and write mini-essays as a means of preparing the thinking and writing process before attempting a finished product. (A more detailed discussion of the steps of the entire writing process is presented in Activity 3.)

Prewriting

Prewriting consists of those activities in which the students experience something as a catalyst for writing. It is a time for reflection, doodling, clustering, outlining, note taking, or just sitting and thinking. These prewriting activities are designed to stimulate thinking and/or writing that can be incorporated into a large final assignment later. It is the technique used for getting started. It is showing a picture, reading a short article, bringing an object into class, playing some music, asking a question, writing some ideas, playing with phrases, free flow writing. Many of the activities in this book are prewriting activities designed to introduce a theme, encourage further investigation of a theme, prepare for a final examination of a theme, teach a skill to be incorporated into a larger assignment later, or introduce students to a technique.

Writing

Writing needs to be looked at as a process, not as an end product. For students to improve their writing, you need to teach a process, not merely assign more writing. The amount of writing is not nearly as critical as the process from which that writing was created. My students, no matter what the grade level, rarely write more than one page until the latter part of the second semester. The process needs to be understandable and independently usable for students. The intent of this book is to take students through various steps of developing writing techniques that, when learned, can be applied to all types of writing. If you teach the process, the product will surely improve.

Do not allow students to do neat first drafts. When they are writing in class, walk around the room watching students write, giving comments like "This looks too neat, it doesn't show rethinking, reevaluating, rereading." Most effective is having students work on large sheets of construction paper or newsprint so that they can draw arrows, do mini-outlines, cluster, and write phrases, sentences, and paragraphs. It allows them to see the whole picture at once.

Some short assignments should be done in longhand and marked up. Some assignments that get typed should be cut up and rearranged. Some assignments should be turned in with the corrections and editing marks but not actually rewritten. This will show the writing process is merely a second step, not a final step.

Revision

Revision is an essential part of the writing process. It is not a step only for those who fail; it is a step for all writers. Revision is not simply copying over neatly, correcting the spelling and grammatical errors. In *Getting the Words Right*, Theodore Cheney explains that his book is about "writing, rewriting, rereading, reviewing, rethinking, rearranging, repairing, restructuring, reevaluating, editing, tightening, sharpening, smoothing, pruning, polishing, punching up, amending, altering, eliminating, transposing, expanding, condensing, connecting, cohering, unifying, perfecting."

Re(vision) literally means to re(look). This is what we want students to do, to take a fresh look at what they have been writing. The revision process is the most difficult to get students to accept. They need to see it not as a penalty, but as the rethinking and rearranging of ideas and words that must be done in order for the writing to achieve its goal: communication.

Students must first learn that writing badly is a crucial part of learning to write well. First, students need to write—a lot! Peter Elbow in *Writing Without Teachers* explains, "Indeed, regressing and falling apart are a crucial and usually necessary part of any complex learning. Schools tend to emphasize success and thereby undermine learning." Students need to learn that the experiment was not a failure; the results just came out differently than expected. Writing is the process of looking for the right words. Revision is then choosing the right words. As Cheney continues, "75 percent of all revision is eliminating words already written; the remaining 25 percent is improving the words that remain . . . the judgment should always be based on 'does it move the piece forward?'"

• *Writing and Evaluation* •

While assignments can contain creative ambiguity, your method of evaluation must be clear to students. Upon what criteria will you be judging these papers? Making good assignments not only involves creative ambiguity, but it should also include well-constructed questions to be addressed, a clear explanation of the parameters of the topic, and a complete list of criteria of evaluation.

This section develops sequentially from setting objectives, creating clear focus for an assignment, dealing with the issue of length, to developing evaluation guidelines and techniques.

Making the Assignment

Prior to giving assignments you must first identify your objective. If you want to know all the revolutions that have occurred since 1776, it makes more sense to assign a list than a compare/contrast paper. The section on operative words (pages 75–77) will help you frame your assignment, but you must determine the paper's purpose. Are you teaching a theme through writing, introducing a concept, merely trying to elicit more written work from the students, or working on a particular skill? By closely identifying your goal you will probably find that most of the written assignments you have previously assigned as major papers could be reduced to a few paragraphs or a couple of pages.

When an assignment is given, a part of the directions must include the criteria for evaluation. If footnotes count, it must be stated. If the number of quotes is critical, it must be stated. Will correct spelling, neatness, inclusion of a bibliography, creation of illustrations all be expected?

"How long should the paper be?" Have you ever given an assignment in which that was not the first question? Students should not become word counters, wide-margin setters, redundant writers, or quitters prior to attempting the assignment. The objective of the paper determines the process, and the process determines the criteria of evaluation; all three factors should help you in setting length guidelines.

Objective + Process + Criteria of Evaluation = Length

A clearly established objective for an assignment, what process the student should go through to complete the assignment, and what the criteria will be to evaluate that assignment should inherently tell the student how long the paper must be to complete the assignment successfully.

Take, for example, an assignment to define *love* by looking it up in the dictionary and in a psychology textbook glossary and writing these two definitions on a sheet of paper with a long sentence definition of the student's own. The paper will be graded on the neatness, spelling, and accuracy of the two sources and on the quality of analysis and synthesis of the student's original sentence. This objective clearly tells the student the length of the paper. Take an assignment to compare the revolution in France of 1789 with that of America in 1776 and to consult at least five primary sources. The paper will be based upon original analysis of primary sources and the student's accurate presentation of factual material, along with standard editing and writing criteria. This tells students that this assignment is a much longer one than the first.

The words you use to make your assignment thus become critical, and your operative words will help determine length of the paper. If you have asked students to *compare* and *contrast,* then two presentations are required. A response to an assignment to *define* will be much shorter than one to an assignment to *analyze.* You'll expect more from an assignment to *discuss* than from one to *list.* Assignments with directions that simply read "Write about ..." offer nothing to students.

Establish a clear relationship among the objectives of the assignment, the time allowed for the assignment, and the length of the paper. By spending more time explaining what is required in a paper based on the operative word in the assignment (see pages 75–77 for a detailed explanation of operative words), you will give the student a clearer picture of what is expected in such an assignment. By clearly listing the elements of the assignment, you help clarify expectations of length. Use a series of prewriting assignments as a part of the overall project. Students are collecting material that will eventually become part of the total length of the assignment.

If you have conscientiously done all this, and students still ask, "Yeah, but, like, how long does it have to like be?" I suggest you give some ranges. Reexplain the nature of the assignment, and then set some minimum standard of length. With shorter assignments, I have had success with telling students to spend 5 minutes in just thinking, then 5–10 minutes clustering or outlining and reviewing their notes, followed by 20–30 minutes actually writing with a 5–10 minute revision period. This is a perfect way to personalize assignments. (Personalizing as to individualizing: individualization is to give each student a specific and unique assignment to meet that student's needs; personalization is giving the whole class the same assignment and then having different expectations of completion for each child.)

When evaluating a student's paper, judge the depth more than the overall length. If sufficient depth is achieved, the necessary length will be there. Thus you would say, "You do not cite enough examples on this point," or "You do not have enough background information on this point to draw such a conclusion," rather than "Not long enough." It is important for students to understand that you *read* the papers—that you don't weigh them or measure them for the purpose of assigning a grade.

Students rarely make a connection between due dates and the actual time needed to do an assignment. An assignment due long in the future is always preferable to them. Thus, developmental assignments seem to answer many of the problems of length. Developmental assignments are writing assignments such as title alternatives, purpose statements, working bibliographies, research cards, introductions, first chapter, and conclusion which are all to be handed in, evaluated and returned prior to reading and evaluating the final paper. Developmental assignments ensure quality papers.

How are you going to find time to read papers twice? Doing detailed reading of a rough draft is much more valuable to the student (and eventually more time-saving to you) than is the thorough reading of the final paper. If you do a complete reading of the rough draft, you can skim the final paper, checking only to make sure that problems identified in the initial reading have been rectified. Before students get so involved in the paper that they have no opportunity or desire to revise, alert them to problems so that they can finish the paper on time with successful results. Allow students to choose when they are done with their revision process. Assign a grade as the paper stands; if they choose to continue to work on it, let them. Require a certain percentage of papers be turned in for grades out of the total number of papers assigned.

Guidelines for Evaluation

If the writing assignment has clearly specified the goal and the criteria for evaluation, evaluating papers using these processes merely becomes a matter of procedure. The major problem, according to most teachers, is finding the time to read and evaluate these papers adequately and effectively. In order to help rectify this situation, you need to determine exactly what your objectives are for evaluation of each assignment. If your only objective for each paper you assign is to levy a grade, you are not fully using all the potential of the evaluation process. Some assignments should be used as a means to introduce material; for those, a grade is not only unnecessary but unfair. Some assignments will allow students to put information to use; other assignments may be used to demonstrate competency in an area, and some will be used to evaluate a student's mastery of information you have presented.

Not all writing should be graded, not all writing should be evaluated, and you need not read all writing. What is more critical is that students write. Specific skills for evaluating papers will be covered on pages 14–18.

You need to decide which information you are presenting for introduction, which for the development of competency, and which for mastery. These factors should play a role in your evaluation of a student's writing. For example, you may expect students to master Woodrow Wilson's Fourteen Points, or you may expect competency in describing his plan for getting the United States Senate to ratify the Versailles Treaty. On the other hand, you may want students only to relate how Wilson's illness played a part in his failure to get the treaty ratified. Thus your objectives affect your criteria for assigning grades in each of these cases.

Regurgitation of information as the primary goal of writing limits the future growth of students in acquiring both content knowledge and writing skills. Rather than asking, "What is the information?" you should ask, "What is the significance of the information?"

How much evaluation will be done on technical writing skills and how much on the content of the paper? As Marge Frank states in *If You're Trying to Teach Kids How to Write, You've Gotta Have This Book!*, "Good writing is based on a healthy friendship between imagination and technique. It can and must be taught without slighting the other."

It is usually easier and less time-consuming to mark the spelling, capitalization, usage, tense agreement, and other mechanical problems than to write detailed substantive comments concerning content. If you focus predominately on technical skills, the result will be you will teach children only to write what they can spell; they will only use a simple sentence structure, they will not choose any topics or approaches that are risky; and most important, they will never learn the joy of writing.

For each assignment a teacher should have an idea based on the assignment's objective, the writing process required, and the means of evaluation—including how much emphasis will be put on technical skills. The closer the assignment approaches the finished product, the more detailed attention there should be to writing mechanics. The more preliminary the assignment, the less the technical skills should be emphasized.

Checklist for Evaluation

In order for the returned papers to be of any use to students, each student in the class should have a permanent list of editorial correction marks which are always to be used by evaluators when editing papers. (See Appendix A, page 187.)

Students should have a notebook specifically for writing. The notebook should have a section for notes, errors from passed-back papers, your discussions on common errors of the class on specific assignments, a place to keep dittos handed out, and finally an assignment section or assignment book.

The evaluator, whether student or teacher, will find the following checklist helpful when conducting an evaluation of a piece of writing.

COMMENTS ON FOCUS: Continue to refer to what the assignment is and how the student is addressing it. A major reason for failed papers is that students don't focus on the assigned topic or question.

MARKING PAPERS: The most beneficial technique I've found to evaluate papers is to make the evaluation a learning experience and ask questions about the writing. A student is likely to get involved by a comment such as "Does this sentence logically follow the first?" or "Are you certain that it was Hemingway who said this?," or even "Is this word used (or spelled) correctly?"

Offer corrective measures using questions. For example, "Could this point be substantiated with some additional evidence?," or "Would a date help clarify this sentence?," or "Would *list, set,* or *alternative* be a better word here?" This provides the student with some framework for correcting problems in the papers.

With papers that appear to be total failures, your evaluation should focus on one or two major problems throughout the papers, rather than on every mistake.

Make positive comments as well as offer corrections. The final comment must make the student want to move forward with the writing.

Identify how a paper has made progress over the student's earlier papers, and provide an objective to work on in the next effort.

EVALUATING CONCLUSIONS: Determine that conclusions mention no points that are not addressed in the main body.

Reinforce the point that conclusions should be the result of the evidence presented.

Reinforce the point that small conclusions based on a large amount of evidence should be arrived at rather than the reverse, which is what is so typically taught and written.

RETURNING PAPERS: Return papers as quickly as possible so that the work is still fresh in the students' minds. You may want to stagger the days on which assignments are due from each class so you only have one set of papers to deal with at a time.

Before handing back papers, orally comment to the class on common problems in the papers and give some general suggestions that would benefit all students. These comments should be recorded in their notebooks.

Collect all papers to create a portfolio of the students' work. This provides you with a wholistic way of looking back at their work and development.

I have a notebook with a page for each student. Each time I read a paper, I write the name of the assignment, the date, and a few brief phrases about the students problems and progress. It is a valuable source when holding conferences and in writing evaluations; it takes perhaps 15 seconds per paper.

Evaluation Techniques

The first question you need to ask yourself is, "Why am I reading this piece of writing?" Are you reading to edit, grade, measure learning, offer advice for revision, or as a means to prepare the student to do the next step of a large writing assignment? What you look for and thus comment on will be different in each case.

"Criticism: the art of considering merits and demerits and judging accordingly." This is not a definition that students would accept. To them offering criticism is only telling them what is wrong with their work. At the beginning of the year you need to talk about how personal the act of writing is and how writers share who they are. You need to establish a rapport with your class so that students look at the editing process as a learning, communication experience. They need to be convinced of the three stages of writing and that this is how all successful writers revise. By asking questions such as, "Could you tell the reader exactly your objective in the first paragraph?" rather than "first paragraph unfocused," you help establish the rewriting environment.

We talk a great deal in my class about developing writer's thick skin. We emphasize over and over that good writing only comes from addressing weak writing. We don't allow people to editorialize before reading their work with "This isn't very good, but here goes . . ." I often ask students for a really bad sentence from their essay as an example of what we are working on in class. The more students accept the writing class as a place of growth through constructive criticism, the more they will become writers. The continual attention to establishing and maintaining this environment has been one of the most important aspects of my writing classroom.

The most successful means of communicating ways to improve a student's writing is through individual writing conferences. Before you throw up your hands saying you don't have time, read some of the basic techniques listed here, and most importantly, get the definitive work on conferencing with students by Donald Graves entitled *Writing: Teachers and Children at Work* (see bibliography). Forty seconds per child will reap you untold success.

Students must see you as an editor, a co-author, a helper. You are the person who is going to help them write more self-satisfying work. If students see you only as the person who grades writing, it will be a long and unsatisfactory trip before the writing gets better.

Following are a number of techniques for you to use to teach students how to revise their work. Many of these techniques can be done orally or directly written on the students' papers.

Peter Elbow in his classic book *Writing Without Teachers* gives writing teachers some suggestions on how to talk to students about their work. He recommends referring to their work in terms of voices. Tell the student that the piece seems to be "shouting, whining, whispering, lecturing sternly, droning, speaking abstractly, defending, preaching, guessing." He suggests that another way of identifying the student's major focus is to refer to the work in terms of weather such as "foggy, sunny, gusty, drizzling, cold, clear, crisp or muggy."

It is beneficial to point out to a student the motion of their piece. The words *marching, climbing, crawling, rolling along, tiptoeing, strolling, sprinting, jumping* have proved successful.

Students can often understand what is wrong with a paper, know what your comments on their writing mean, but can't "hear" a good paper. Students need to know why another student's paper is more successful. Read a successful paper to them, and have them jot a few notes or create a cluster of ideas or lead a discussion on what the differences are between this paper and theirs.

Students should also read their own papers aloud as an editing technique. Those listening are to take notes. Hearing a paper read aloud helps students find errors that would have gone unnoticed in a silent reading. In groups of four to six, students can read their papers while the group takes detailed, specific notes. The author must read the paper exactly as written—no oral revises. When each student is through reading, the group provides input for the eventual revision. Having the group ask questions rather than make statements creates a much more positive environment for revisions.

One technique for evaluating papers is simply to fold a sheet of paper into the same number of vertical columns as there are pages of the student's paper. Each horizontal line of a column corresponds to a line on the student's paper. Keep the folded paper side-by-side with the student's; as you find mistakes in the student's paper you make a mark on the corresponding line of the folded sheet. When you have finished correcting the paper in this manner, you have two options. One is to keep this sheet, return the original paper to the student for revision, and use your sheet as a guide to evaluating their revision skills. The other option is to give the correction sheet to the student as a guide for finding mistakes. This spares students the trauma of a red-inked paper, and also makes it their responsibility to locate and correct the mistakes. Either of these approaches makes paper evaluation a learning experience for the student.

Another technique for correcting papers is geared to the ability of the individual students. The more help they need, the more specific you should be. Assume you are correcting for spelling (any technical skill works the same way). If the student is the worst speller in the county, you underline the misspelled word and write the correct spelling above. If the student is only the worst speller in the city, perhaps you merely underline the misspelled word expecting the student to correct it. A more proficient speller would merely have "sp" written at the beginning of the line that contains a misspelled word, and the writer would have to find the misspelling. Expert spellers will merely have at the bottom of the page "2-sp" and they will have to reread the work to find the errors. This technique is adaptable to all editing concerns.

A third technique is to evaluate only one skill. For example, you may skim a paper to check the amount of research or the effectiveness of the introduction or how the topic sentence and the conclusion relate. This single area would be the only focus of your comments.

A fourth technique is to get two students to write on related subjects. They read and criticize each other's papers, comparing the similarities and the differences in each other's treatment of the same topic.

The review team is also useful. It not only gets papers thoroughly read but develops positive group interaction. Group experts in spelling, punctuation, usage, brevity, vocabulary, quotes, evidence, and subject matter are chosen. Experts edit only for their errors. Students' papers will be read by many students and few mistakes will go unnoticed. All students can become experts at something (titles for papers, footnote format, bibliography format, or even correct pagination).

It is more important for students to write than to be evaluated constantly. Students learn by writing as well as by reading your comments. You can use short, daily written assignments as a means of developing students' writing skills as well as reviewing or introducing course content.

Too often, however, students don't even bother to read the teacher's comments. That is why I have students keep track of their writing problems in their notebooks. Every ten weeks, students prepare an essay on their present writing problems and areas of improvement.

If you don't feel comfortable beginning a full-fledged conferencing component to your writing program and you haven't time to read through *Writing Without Teachers* or *Writing: Children and Teachers at Work*, perhaps you would be willing to try this simple evaluation activity.

1. Ask students to write about what they are thinking, feeling, wondering, hiding, or worrying about. Explain they are not to be concerned about spelling, neatness or any technical problems. Tell them to get down as many thoughts as possible in five minutes.

2. At the end of five minutes ask students to put their pens down and read what they have written.

3. While they are reading, you walk to each student and read the paper for 20 seconds and then respond for 20 seconds. Use some of the responses suggested by Elbow or create your own statements that give students' a wholistic view of what you have read. Even a single word will do if it is specific: "Focused, powerful, sad, wishful." You can begin reading their paper on any line—any feedback is helpful.

4. After you have conferenced with each student, the students should return to writing.

5. At the end of 3–5 more minutes of writing, have students divide into manageable size groups and read their work aloud. Students may respond for 40 seconds to each work. (Make sure you have already presented your material on criticism.)

You have just personalized your writing program using very little time.

Worksheets for Evaluation

One way to create consistency of evaluation is to use evaluation worksheets. These worksheets could be used for a student's self-evaluation, peer evaluation, or evaluation of particular types of writing assignments.

Peter Elbow gives a very simple, brief worksheet form that is positive, effective, and enlightening for the students to respond to each other's work or their own. This worksheet is not only helpful but is a powerful learning experience for student editors—their writing improves as a result of conscientious editing. Editorial feedback helps writers answer the question "Are people receiving the writing as I intended it?" (See page 143.) Teachers can also use this worksheet effectively.

In addition to this evaluation worksheet, you may want to develop evaluation worksheets for specific kinds of assignments. Worksheets 2 and 3 are for self-evaluation, peer evaluation, and a general editing checklist worksheet.

This book includes other worksheets for students to use for evaluating books, articles, television programs, and movies. Students should then attempt these same kinds of writing. See also Activities 104 and 105 (pages 135–138) for some specific recommendations for additional writing assignments in these areas. Each of these worksheets is self-explanatory; directions are given only in special cases.

2. Introducing Writing to Your Class

*C*reating students' enthusiasm about writing and getting them to believe that they can do it effectively and joyously is the first step in teaching the writing process.

The activities in this chapter are designed for you to present information about writers, the writing process, and to encourage students to initially put pen to paper. The activities do not actually teach writing skills; such teaching is in the following chapters.

It was tempting to include a section to convince you to use a journal with your students, but I am going to assume you have read about keeping a journal and are familiar with books that do an excellent job of presenting this valuable idea, as well as strategies for using the student journal. Refer to the bibliography if you would like additional references on this topic. I do, however, encourage you to use a journal of some kind in your classroom.

• *Writers and Writing* •

The purpose of this chapter is to introduce students to the writing process. It is intended to present students with the difference between someone who writes (a skill generally learned in second grade) and a writer (a life-long learning craft). It is in presenting this material that the tone will be set with your class. Do not rush it; establish trust and enthusiasm. These activities promote discussion and interaction rather than actual writing tasks.

Students need to learn about what writers believe about writing. Most students have little, if any, identification with writers and the writing process. Students don't believe real writing is something they do. Below are the thoughts of three writers on the writing process. All three writers have different purposes, but the concern of all is to get quality writing from students through a supportive environment. These first three activities will help lay the groundwork for convincing students that they, too, can follow this process and be writers. The chapter ends with an activity by which you acquire initial writing samples from your class.

ACTIVITY 1: WRITER OR JUST WRITING

*D*onald Murray in *A Writer Teaches Writing* explains what a writer does. What he says is worth sharing with your students in discussing both content and style. He can be excused for the exclusive use of the masculine pronoun; I am sure Murray feels women are also writers. (For an excellent treatment of sexist language and how to handle the male pronoun, Casey Miller and Kate Swift's *The Handbook of Nonsexist Writing* has not only helped me become a nonsexist writer, but has improved my writing overall.)

Students may not understand all of this or even know, perhaps, how it applies to them. But they should hear a certain harmony in the words. The writing should sound good to them. Begin to train the ear; it is the best editor around.

Scope: The purpose of this activity is to present to students Donald Murray's view of what a writer does and elicit discussion about the writing process. It can take from 20 minutes to an entire period. It involves leading a discussion from material presented below and having students fill out a worksheet.

Process: Give students Worksheet 8 (this worksheet along with 9 and 10 should become permanent parts of the student's binder) and ask them to complete the outline with information you and the class discuss based upon the quotation below. You may simply want to just read the quotation as is. You may want to stop after each major point and have discussion. You may want students to copy the boldface material on the worksheet. You may want them to cluster their ideas as the discussion develops. You may want a formal outline. The worksheet is a guide to discussion. How to use it effectively is up to you.

"The Writer Sees. *The writer sees what we do not see in what we all see. He finds the ordinary extraordinary and old truths new.*

"He has the gifts of reception and perception. He appears to receive more impressions than other men, but in their

confusion he discovers patterns. He has ability to be specific, to see with precision and accuracy. He disbelieves to believe, destroys to rebuild. The writer has to impose order on disorder.

"The Writer Writes. The writer has the courage or the compulsion to reveal himself. He commits himself.

"The writer is obsessed with form, but not as an empty vessel into which he pours meaning. He knows he has to have something worth saying. What he wants to say determines which tool he will use. For him words are never isolated from meaning, grammar segregated from subject, rhetoric divorced from purpose.

"The writer works through specifics to generalizations and back. Hemingway said writing is architecture, not interior decoration. The writer builds with specific details, writing by selection. He forms, fits, shapes, and wastes. He knows the value of what he completes might properly be judged by what he has ruthlessly tossed away.

"He respects brevity, knowing its challenge, and attempts to cut away from complexity to clarity. His goal is simplicity— the flight of the seagull. He seeks the least complicated way of expressing the most complicated idea. The writer tries to see and then make the reader see. He does not want to tell but to show. He believes he is successful when he is invisible, when the reader discovers the subject himself.

"The Writer revises. Art is beyond craft, but art grows out of craft. Craft is the calculation which turns inspiration into creation.

"The craftsman writes by rewriting, and he revises by re-seeing and re-thinking. He seeks the inspiration of the writing desk. He understands that writing is a way of perceiving, a method of discovery, and refinement and synthesis and clarification.

"The writer dreams of art, but he works at craft."

ACTIVITY 2: TOOLS OF THE WRITER

*P*aul Kalkstein's *Good Writing* identifies eleven simple elements that the writer uses to create exciting prose. Again, this information is a lot to handle in one lesson, but it provides the background to which you will return again and again.

Scope: The purpose of this activity is to present to students the practical skills and techniques, according to Paul Kalkstein, that a writer uses so that the list of skills can become a checklist for evaluating writing. The activity generally takes the entire period. It involves leading a discussion from material below and students filling out a worksheet.

Process: Distribute Worksheet 9 and ask students to fill it out in similar fashion as in Activity 1 as you and the class discuss the following passage. Again, you may wish to read this passage aloud or to present some of its information and then stimulate discussion. How you use the material is not nearly as critical as using it.

1. Unity. Unity in writing is faithful to a central idea. In a sentence, unity is the expression of a single complete thought; in a paragraph, unity is the development of the topic idea; in a longer piece, unity is development of the thesis statement.

2. Originality. Trite phrases, dead metaphors, old slogans— these bore a reader and leave no impression. On the other hand, a fresh, emphatic structure, or an arresting metaphor or a sharp word used properly in a new context arouses the interest of a reader and makes the writer's idea memorable.

3. Emphasis. Effective emphasis on the focal idea or ideas in a composition makes the reader pause to think. A requisite for emphatic writing is the ability to discriminate between important ideas and subordinate or supporting ideas.

4. Diction. Diction in writing is the writer's choice of words.

5. Development. *The length* (of a piece of writing) *depends on how much the writer's audience needs to know. The writing should be economical, of course, but it should contain enough information to communicate effectively to the audience.*

6. Conciseness. *A concise statement does not elaborate upon an idea beyond what is necessary to communicate to an audience.*

7. Coherence. *Coherent writing sticks together. It proceeds clearly from one point to another, as it develops the central, or unifying, idea.*

8. Clarity. *Writers achieve clarity through precision, and they achieve precision through good hard work.*

9. Audience. *Writers must think about who will read what they write. Sometimes, as in advertising, a writer's audience is the first and most important consideration.*

10. Active voice. *The passive* (voice) *slows down the pace of the prose and clouds the meaning.*

11. Sources. *Often good writers borrow from sources* (the writing of others). *These borrowings serve two chief functions: (1) use of a source can buttress a writer's argument by drawing on the expertise of another and (2) borrowing a witty line or a choice turn of phrase from another writer can enliven one's prose and also provide a refreshing variety of voice or point of view.* (These ideas provide an appropriate opportunity briefly to discuss plagiarism and direct and indirect quotations.)

ACTIVITY 3: THE WRITING PROCESS

*I*n the following activity, I have adapted the terminology of Marge Frank (*If You Teach Kids How To Write, You've Gotta Have This Book*) to fit my definitions of the writing process.

Scope: This activity should provide students with a clear understanding of the necessary steps when developing an essay. The activity generally takes about half the period. It involves leading a discussion from material below and students filling out a worksheet.

Process: Distribute Worksheet 10 and have students fill out the skeleton outline with more detailed information as a result of your presentation and the class discussion. This material can be discussed as in Activities 1 and 2.

1. Motivation. Generally I want something to happen in class before students write. A movie is shown, a record is played, a picture is tacked up, a trip is taken, a speech is heard, some research is done, a question is asked, an activity is participated in—some experience should take place which triggers the creative juices.

2. Collecting Impressions. This is the time for students to do clustering, outlining, key word writing, sketching: transferring what is in their heads to paper.

3. Rough Draft. Student's goal is to "get something down." The writing should be without concern for technical skills, organization or direction. After 5–10 minutes of writing, students should have a clearer idea of where they are going and begin to refocus the work as they write. Working fast, working messy, and working on large sheets of paper are all appropriate.

4. Rereading. Students finish their work and go back to reread the piece for sense and readability. They now need to see the piece as a whole, not just individual sentences or paragraphs.

5. Sharing. With peer partners, students read their work to each other, with the peer offering feedback.

6. Editing. This is when the reshuffling process should take place. Scissors and glue, with lots of cross-outs, arrows, and connection lines is the best way to do it. This is not writing over; it is rethinking, revising, and reconsidering to give the piece more power, more impact.

7. Mechanics Check. Before final revision, students make a final spelling, grammar, syntax, verb agreement, and other technical-areas check.

8. Final Draft. Now students can revise or type the final draft.

9. Presenting. Pieces are "published" so as to celebrate writing.

ACTIVITY 4: THE WRITING SAMPLE

*A*fter having presented what writers do and how they do it, you can get writing samples from the class. Picking something rather esoteric so that they do not have any past writing or experiences on which to draw is a good idea. You can observe their thinking process as well as their writing process at work.

Scope: This activity is designed to begin to introduce the concept of ambiguity in the writing process. (See pages 6–7 for a discussion of the concept of assignments with ambiguity.) You are placing students in a unique writing environment and asking them to draw on their own imagination and skills to produce an essay.

This activity takes an entire period and involves a homework assignment. It involves leading a discussion from material below and students filling out a worksheet.

Materials: You will need a non-narrated film. I strongly recommend "Dream of the Wild Horses," "Solo," "Junkyard," "Fog," "Snow," "What is Art?" Any film library will have some short, non-narrated film that will serve your purpose. You could also use a large poster, a photograph, music, or a similar stimulant.

Process: Ask students to divide a sheet of paper into six sections and label them: *see, hear, taste, touch, smell,* and *feel* (emotions). As each of their senses is stimulated by watching the film, they are to write words or phrases under each of the appropriate sense columns. The idea is to create a senses dictionary stimulated by the film. These words are then used in their writing assignment based on the film.

After viewing the film, give students time to finish up their senses dictionary and then begin writing. The assignment is to be completed at home.

You may wish to pose a general question for the students such as "Which of your senses was most touched by this film and why? Cite specific examples." But merely asking them to *respond* will give you more information about student's writing. You are not clarifying this assignment because you want to see what the students can do without instruction.

Creating Images:
• From Words to Paragraphs •

For communication to take place through writing, the writing must be specific, vigorous, clear, and concise. The activities in this chapter follow a logical development from a simple idea to a sentence, to a better sentence, to a sentence with purpose.

As with all activities in this book, whenever your students finish an in-class written or oral activity you may want to assign homework, or have students redo the activity in order to fully understand the concept fully. Remember to keep the assignments brief. Most of the concepts can be absorbed with a couple of review tasks. Two or three well-done sentences are much preferable to 20 or 30 sentences done only to complete the homework.

ACTIVITY 5: WRITING A SENTENCE THAT COMMUNICATES

Scope:
The purpose of this activity is to teach students the goals of clarity, brevity, and specificity through specific examples. It takes 10–15 minutes. Discussion, teacher modeling sentence on the board, and student revision are all encompassed in this activity.

Process:	Write on the board the following sentence and have students revise it on their paper, seeking clarity, brevity, and specificity in their writing:

Maximum affection is hereby implied.

Ask students to read revisions aloud. Finally share with them the clear, brief, specific revision below:

I love you.

Write the second example on the board and follow the same procedure:

Conflagration, conflagration! Hasten hither the mechanical device used for the suppression of combustion.

Determine if the student responses are similar to:

Fire! Call for a fire truck.

ACTIVITY 6: WRITING A SENTENCE WITH SPECIFIC IMAGES

*C*reating images is the goal of many writers—to have the reader experience what the writer has experienced, not by telling but by showing.

Scope:	The purpose of this activity is to have students learn to write clear, specific, brief sentences with vigorous prose that communicate images. Stress that you are not looking merely for a description but for a sentence that has a point, makes a statement.
	This activity will take most of the period. It again involves oral presentation, oral revision, and students writing.
Process:	Ask students which is more specific: plant, flower, or rose.
	At the top of the board write "vehicle" and ask students to follow as you progressively write a more specific image.

vehicle—car—Chevrolet—Chevrolet Barretta—
Chevrolet Barretta convertible

Now ask students to take the final phrase and write it down on a piece of paper. Tell them they will be adding to this phrase to create an image. (You should continue to develop your own sentence on the board so students can see you struggle, edit, problem solve, and make decisions as you write.)

First, have students add the sense of sight to the phrase. Ask what color is the car?

blue(?) Chevrolet Barretta convertible

To this phrase, have students add the sense of touch. Ask: What is the texture of the car?

dented(?) blue Chevrolet Barretta convertible

Next, have students add sound. Ask: What do they hear from the car?

sputtering(?) tattered, blue Chevrolet Barretta convertible

Finally, ask students to add a verb to their phrase. Explain they can add whatever other words are needed to their basic phrase to make a complete sentence and they may wish to rearrange the words in some manner.

The blue Chevrolet Barretta with its dented body, coughing and sputtering, began its daily task of car- pooling the kids to school.

Students have now created a concrete image. Have students read their images aloud.

ACTIVITY 7: WRITING A SENTENCE WITH THE RIGHT IMAGE

You may want to restate the point that the difference between a writer and someone who merely writes is the ability to create images. Joseph Conrad wrote, "My task is by the power of the written word to make you hear, to make you feel—it is above all—to make you see."

The writer's job is to have the reader share the writer's experience. Don't tell the experience, show it. If readers come to the same conclusion (experience) that the writer had without telling them, the writer has communicated effectively. Continually use the concept SHOW, DON'T TELL when evaluating students' writing and insist that the writing make a statement. For example, a paragraph describing a homeless person might move toward a point about the hopelessness of the situation rather than being merely a description.

Now that students have sequentially developed an image, they should be ready to develop better images.

Scope: The purpose of this activity is to introduce students to the difference between LOOKING and SEEING as it relates to creating images through writing. It should take the entire period. It involves both leading a discussion and students doing some brief writing.

Process: Initiate a discussion with students by asking them the difference between seeing and looking.

Ask students to look out the window and describe what they see. Explain that everyone can list the images they see out the window. Ask who sees "how the light reflects off the leaves dappling the tree trunk creating the only beauty in all the city" (or a sentence geared for the view from your windows).

(Your discussion on LOOKING and SEEING can be carried over into the difference between HEARING and LISTENING. Very often what passes for listening is only hearing the moment when the other person stops so you can begin speaking. Listening is absorbing the speaker's message.)

Next ask students randomly to pick a concrete noun (car, tree, book, flower, desk, hair, etc.).

Ask students to add a color word in front of or behind their noun: *silver hair*.

Next ask students to add a touch word in front of or behind their newly created phrase (if a taste, smell, or sound word works better tell students to use it): *lifeless silver hair*.

Have students read their phrases aloud. Have the class respond to these images.

Have students repeat this activity as often as time permits. The important point is to stress how images are created. Have students strive for the unique, not the trite. The sentence must work. They need to listen to what they say and write. Have they made statements with these phrases? Which ones work and why?

ACTIVITY 8: WRITING A SENTENCE WITH ACTION VERBS

*T*o become a sentence, a phrase needs a verb. Students need to learn that the best writing is done with strong nouns and verbs. If you are usually forced to teach grammar independently of writing or literature, here is a "teachable moment" for integrating grammar study with writing by focusing on nouns, verbs, adverbs and adjectives.

Scope: The purpose of this activity is teach students that strong sentences are created with strong nouns and verbs. The activity should take 10–15 minutes. It involves a teacher-led discussion, modeling some sentences on the board, and students doing oral revision.

Process: Point out the importance of choosing verbs to create images. Discuss the difference between *put, shoved, delicately placed,* and *jammed in.* Ask the students to what nouns these verbs or verb phrases might refer (flowers, books?).

Write a simple sentence on the board. The less creative the better. You may find it easier to use the following example here, rather than your own; this sentence is used in the next two activities:

The boy went after the bus.

Ask students to make the sentence stronger in action by changing the verb.

The boy ran after the bus.

Have students go the other direction and make the action weaker.

The boy limped after the bus.

Discuss with students how the sentence tone changes by changing verbs. Point out stronger is not better than weaker. Each fits a specific situation. Ask the students to change the verb a number of times, from stronger to weaker, and vice-versa.

Read aloud a number of sentences. Ask students to respond orally, making the sentence stronger and then weaker until they demonstrate understanding of the power of a verb to focus the sentence.

ACTIVITY 9: FINDING THE RIGHT NOUNS AND VERBS

Scope:
*T*he purpose of this activity is to develop further the concepts of individual perception, creating images, and choosing proper nouns and verbs. This activity takes 15–25 minutes and should ask students to practice writing some sentences at home. It involves teacher discussion, modeling sentences on the board, and students writing some of their own sentences.

Have students keep their work from Activities 9 and 10 and 11 as it will be used for other activities.

Process:
Explain that an image can be radically altered by changing the nouns and verbs. To demonstrate this concept, write on the board the first model sentence used in the previous activity.

The boy went after the bus.

Now revise the sentence changing the noun and verb.

The cheerleader sprinted toward the bus.

Point out to students that the first example is merely a sentence; the second is an image.

Call on students to orally revise the original sentence by changing the noun and verb.

The punk rocker sauntered to the bus.

Discuss how their new sentences (and yours) create images based upon the clear nouns and verbs that are used.

ACTIVITY 10: CHANGING THE FOCUS OF A SENTENCE

Scope: *T*he purpose of this activity is to show not only that the image can be altered by a few carefully selected words, but that inference of a sentence can be changed. The activity takes about 15 minutes. It involves modeling sentences on the board and students practicing writing sentences at home and/or orally in class.

Process: Write on the board the model sentence from Activity 8.

The boy went after the bus.

Tell to students that you are going to create a better image by revising the sentence.

The cheerleader sprinted toward the bus.

Now show students how you can change the focus and inference of the sentence by adding a phrase to clarify.

The cheerleader sprinted toward the bus, hoping everyone would see his new squad sweater.

Point out that this revised sentence creates an entirely different image than the original sentence or even the revised second sentence. The purpose for sprinting to the bus and who the cheerleader was both grab the attention of the reader.

The punk rocker sauntered to the bus.
The punk rocker sauntered to the bus amidst cheers for having just pulled a student to safety.

Discuss with students which sentences are best and why. Ask which sentences created stronger images. Finally, have students revise some of their previous sentences utilizing the same technique.

ACTIVITY 11: BUILDING POWER IN A SENTENCE

Scope: *T*he purpose of this activity is to teach students the sequential approach of writing a strong sentence by moving from a noun to a phrase, to an image. The activity takes 20–30 minutes.

This activity involves the teacher modeling sentences on the board, oral revision, and students writing sentences in class. Repeating this activity as homework is a good assignment. It cannot be overly stressed that you want statements, sentences with point, not merely description.

Process: Write the word rose on the board and ask students to do the same on their paper. (Complete all of these steps on the board so that you can model the work for the class.)

Have students write a four word sentence using rose as a noun.

The rose wilted today.

Now have students add to this sentence where the rose is.

The garden rose wilted today.

Next, revise this sentence and add more description to create more of an image.

The forlorn garden rose wilted early this morning.

Add a strong action verb to the sentence.

The forlorn garden rose expired early this morning.

Finally, revise to create a strong image which makes a statement.

The forlorn rose, diseased by toxic water, was the final rose to die in the garden early this morning.

Have students share their image sentences. The rest of the class should listen carefully and offer comments about which images affect them, which are unclear, which are powerful and why.

~~~~~~~~~~

ACTIVITY 12: ONE TWO-PART SENTENCE IS WORTH TWO PICTURES

*T*his next activity is designed for you to give the instructions in class and have the students do the work at home. Your presentation should refer back to the sentences created in Activity 10 in which an image was changed by the final phrasing of the sentence.

Scope: The purpose of this activity is to have students visually depict their sentences to understand how powerful images can be created with words. Presenting the directions (and examples if you wish) for this assignment and referring back to the past work they did in Activity 10 takes about 10 minutes.

Process: Tell students that they will be writing a sentence which is designed to grab the reader because the final part of the sentence takes the reader in a new and unexpected (yet logical) direction. They will be cutting out pictures from magazines which will illustrate the first and second part of their sentence.

Give students an example. For the first part of the sentence use a picture of a man smoking a cigarette while riding his horse.

The open range challenges this cowboy daily. . . .

The second picture for the final part of the sentence is of a man in a hospital with multiple tubes coming out of him and massive machines hooked up to his body. The final part of the sentence reads:

. . . but today, fighting cancer is a much greater challenge for him.

Students are to paste these two pictures on a large piece of paper with the appropriate part of the sentence written under each picture. They visually see how such a sentence leads the reader down one path and then creates a tremendous effect by changing direction.

Students are to orally/visually share their sentence in class. (This makes for a strong bulletin board display.)

Another example: A picture of a happy family at local fast food restaurant.

Fast food is. . . .

Second picture, a burned and slashed rain forest.

. . . quickly frying our rain forests.

The two parts of the sentence should flow smoothly together creating a dynamic compare/contrast set of images. It should not read like two sentences merely pasted together. This activity helps reinforce the concept of writing statements, not just description. Give special praise to those sentences without conjunctions to tie the two clauses.

ACTIVITY 13: SENSES DICTIONARIES

Scope: The purpose of this activity is to have students learn the multitude of words available to them related to the senses. Students will create senses dictionaries that can become their own thesaurus.

This activity could take as little as 15–20 minutes to complete or could be extended to an entire class. It is done in class and involves giving students directions and time to write in class.

Process: Divide the class into six groups and give each of them a different sense on which to focus: hearing, seeing, touching, smelling, tasting. You may wish to add feeling (emotions) although it is not traditionally regarded as a sense. Have each group list as many nouns, verbs, adjectives as they can under each heading. Stress that the goal is quantity. Have them choose words they like to use or would like to use when writing or talking.

When the activity seems to be dying, collect each group's work and quickly make photocopies so that each student has a Senses Dictionary. If you don't have quick access to a machine, the work can be handed out the next day, or students can merely read each other's work in groups.

Have students study this dictionary and become familiar with the words in each section. They may want to discuss why a word is in one section rather than another or could be in more than one column. This dictionary can be used for future writing activities.

ACTIVITY 14: CREATING SENTENCES INSPIRED BY SITUATIONS

Scope:
*T*he purpose of this activity is for students to demonstrate all the skills and techniques they have learned from Activities 1–13. It is designed to be presented in class and done as homework. Students should save this assignment as it will be used in Activity 15.

Process:
Pass out Worksheet 11 and explain to students that they are to demonstrate how to write image sentences. Students are being presented with a situation. Their job is to think about the situation as a writer (unique perception of the ordinary) and to write a sentence with vigorous prose, brevity, specificity, and clarity. Urge students to use their Senses Dictionary.

(You may wish to create your own worksheet of situations that is more suited to your teaching situation. The goal is to get students writing immediately rather than spending time thinking about what to write.)

Have students share their best sentence the next class period and listen carefully for images, statements, strong nouns and verbs, unique perception. Have they made statements, not just descriptions? Discuss with each author.

ACTIVITY 15: RIGHT NOUN, RIGHT VERB, RIGHT IMAGE, RIGHT POWER, WRITE A PARAGRAPH

*A*ll of the sentences that have been created so far have gone beyond mere description. Each of the sentences they write must have a point, a purpose, must make a statement. If they haven't achieved this yet, repeat some of the earlier assignments. If you have only done a few examples in each section, the students will not mind doing a few more.

Scope: The purpose of the final writing activity in this section provides students the opportunity to use what they have learned about writing sentences with images and purpose and to create a paragraph using the same techniques.

Limit students to *three* sentences. As Mark Twain wrote, "If I had more time, I would have written a shorter letter."

This activity is designed to have the directions given in class and the assignment done as homework, but the class period can be utilized for writing.

Process: Have students choose the one sentence from Worksheet 11 they want to develop into a paragraph. Remind them to utilize all that they have learned so far and to limit themselves to three sentences. They are to keep in mind that the paragraph must go beyond description; it must have a point to make, a purpose.

Have students share their work with the class and get class responses to the paragraphs. (This is a good activity for the peer evaluation technique/worksheets described earlier on pages 12–19.) Save these paragraphs as you will use them with activities in the section on figurative language.

(I like to end this section by reading one of my favorite pieces of literature that shows unique perception. Surely you have one, so use yours. But Richard Brautigan's "Kool-Aid Wino" from his *Trout Fishing in America* is unbeatable. This takes about five minutes to read. Discuss with students some of the images Brautigan creates. This reading and discussion leads directly into the next section on figurative language.)

• *Figurative Language* •

ACTIVITY 16: METAPHOR, SIMILE, PERSONIFICATION

The next step to improving the impact of students' images is the use of figurative language: simile, metaphor, personification. All three are comparisons. Simile makes a soft comparison using the words *like* or *as*: "The man eats like a pig." Metaphor makes the comparison saying the one is the other: "That guy is a real pig." Personification gives human qualities to inanimate objects, as Theodore Cheney says, "attributing life to the lifeless": "Fear walked over to the three sleepers and grabbed them simultaneously." Giving human qualities to animals is anthropomorphism: "Spot's eyes could see into the depth of my soul."

Scope: The purpose of this activity is to introduce to students some of the terms of figurative language and have them begin practicing writing them. Students will learn that the use of figurative language can help create even stronger images than they have previously written.

This activity takes three class periods and involves homework assignments. It will require oral writing, modeling of sentences, students writing in class, and homework assignments.

Process: Define the words *simile, metaphor,* and *personification* for the students (you probably will also want to add *anthropomorphism).* Have students write an example of each and share them orally.

Listen to make sure that they are comparing one object to another using a common characteristic. "Bob is as tall as an orange" has no common characteristic being compared. Reiterate that you are not looking for "tall as a giraffe," "big as a house," "eats like a pig," or "red as a rose." What you are looking for is unique perception that works. Make sure the comparisons are clear and easily understood. Too often figurative language is so obscure that it makes no impression on the reader. The point of figurative language is to offer a comparison that will help your reader understand your message.

Have students comment on the other students' work: Which examples work, which are clichés, which are too obscure, and which are new ways of making a point to the reader?

The next part of the activity will help the students learn the technique without worrying about the logic of their sentences. Since similes are the easiest for young writers and metaphors a bit tougher, start with similes.

Ask students to write similes that draw comparisons between the following sets of objects:

a cotton ball and a tire
a pen and a golf ball
an orange and a television
a cry and a fur coat
a freckle and a baseball stadium
a three-ring binder and toothpaste

This activity should bring home to students the idea of comparison using figurative language. Have students write a few metaphors and a few personification sentences and orally share their best ones with the class. (Students usually have the most difficulty with personification. It is movement from literal interpretation to inferential and some have trouble with this.)

For homework have students write ten metaphors, ten personifications and ten similes. These need not be complete sentences, but merely the comparisons. The next class, have students choose their best example from each category and share it with the class. Finally have the students develop each of these best sentences into short paragraphs. This section of the activity can be done in class.

For homework, assign students to take their Writing Sentences Inspired by Situations Worksheet and develop one of their situations into a paragraph that contains one example of each of the above techniques. The next class period, exchange these paragraphs and have peers label each of these techniques in the paragraph. Orally share these paragraphs and discuss with the class

ACTIVITY 17: HYPERBOLE, ALLUSION, METONYMY

Scope: *T*he purpose of this activity is to define the figurative language terms, *hyperbole, allusion,* and *metonymy* and to have students begin using these techniques in their writing.

This activity will take about three class periods. The same process used in Activity 16 will again be used here: oral writing, modeling, student writing, and homework assignments.

Process: Define for students hyperbole (overstatement), litotes (understatement), allusion (a reference to another object, situation, historical event, person which helps clarify a point—it is subtle and casual) and metonymy (using a part of an object or an idea to stand for the whole object or idea).

Mary carried the women's movement on her shoulders as she sued to get a job as a firefighter. (hyperbole)

Nuclear war can ruin a good lunch. (litotes)

Bob appeared Samurai-like as he stood guard at the door. (allusion)

A vicious tongue can ruin a good party. (metonymy)

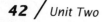

Students should orally or in written form try each of these techniques one at a time, share them orally with the class and then move to the next kind of figurative language.

Assign students ten of each kind of figurative language style. At the next class meeting have students orally share their best examples. Write some of them on the board and work on revising them. A good method is to take some sentences that don't work and model them on the board and create better sentences through revision.

The final task in this activity is to develop a paragraph using these new techniques of figurative language. Donald Murray suggests an interesting question to pose to students: to explain something that they understand as if they don't understand it. His example is: Fireworks is a rainbow at night.

Students should brainstorm a list of topics that are highly sense-oriented and lend themselves to figurative language practice. A thunderstorm, a rainbow, a snow fall, a waterslide, an ocean storm, lightning, are all possible topics.

Have students choose a topic from their brainstorming list and develop a paragraph essay. The essays the students develop should explain a phenomenon as if they do not really know what caused it. The object is to incorporate all the elements of figurative language into the essay.

At the next class meeting have students share their essays orally and engage in discussion or use evaluation techniques and/or worksheets to help the class learn which paragraphs work and why.

ACTIVITY 18: THE RIGHT TWO WORDS

The final judges of whether this works or not are the mind and the ear. Writing on a page is both a visual medium and an auditory one.

More than anything else, good writing is how you put two words together effectively. This activity will help students begin to trust their ear and think about each choice of words more carefully.

Scope: The purpose of this activity is to begin to have students "listen" to their writing and to carefully and consciously choose each word carefully. The activity will begin to help them edit with their ear and not just their pen.

This activity will take two class periods. It will require some modeling, in-class writing, and homework assignments.

Process: On the board write the words: *river* and *stream.* Have students write them on their paper, then ask them to place a modifier in front of each word.

Perhaps students have chosen *raging river* and *meandering stream* or similar choices. Discuss why *raging stream* does not work and *searching stream* does. Why does *meandering stream* create harmony and *torrent creek* does not?

Have students suggest ten nouns, and write them on the board. Have students add a modifier that works: no clichés. Discuss which sentences work and why.

As homework, have students pick ten new nouns, add a modifier to each and then write a complete sentence. Ask them to use figurative language where it will be helpful.

At the next class meeting have students share their best sentences orally and have students comment. Have some students volunteer their worst sentence. Write these on the board and work on revising them so that they do work. The work on the poor sentences is usually the most valuable part of the activity.

ACTIVITY 19: WRITING AND PERCEPTION

Scope: *T*he purpose of this activity is to emphasize that the difference between a writer and someone who writes is perception—seeing the usual in an unusual way. This activity will place students in a situation in which they must use perception to create writing.

This activity will take one period. You will be using in-class writing and oral sharing in this activity.

Material: Grocery bag stapled shut.

Process: Place a stapled-shut large grocery bag on the table in front of the class. Ask each student to write three different explanations of what is in the bag. Each explanation can only be one sentence in length and cannot have a sentence structure of "_____ is in the bag." or "In the bag is _____." That would violate what they have been learning up to now.

Have students orally share their sentences. Determine which work, which don't and why. Identify which sentences used figurative language, which created images. Which helped you visualize exactly what the author described? Which showed rather than told? Who were writers, not just writing? (Any time an activity asks for oral sharing you may want to use some of the techniques and worksheets used in the evaluation section of this book instead. See pages 12–19.)

ACTIVITY 20: WRITING WITH NEW SENSES

Scope: *T*he purpose of this activity is to continue the process of developing unique perception which was begun in Activity 18. Students will be required to use their senses in unusual ways.

This activity will take most of one period. Reading directions to the students and having them write in class are involved in this activity.

Process: Have students answer the following questions on a piece of paper. Read these questions to them one at a time and give them only 10 seconds to respond. Tell them to trust their impressions, their senses.

1. *What does red taste like?*
2. *What does ice-cream sound like?*
3. *What does the smell of rain look like?*
4. *What does fur sound like?*
5. *What does soft look like?*
6. *What does a whisper feel like?*
7. *What does laughing taste like?*

Have students orally share their answers to each question one at a time. What generally happens is students are unable to use one sense to describe another. Look at question 6 for example. Many students will say *quiet*—that is not a feel word, but a sound word. Or for question 7 they will say *happy*—*happy* is not a taste word, *spicy* is.

Discuss why one word is chosen over another and why some words seem to work better than others. Discuss how selection of an exact word is critical to clear writing.

ACTIVITY 21: WRITING A PERSONAL RECIPE

Scope: *T*his activity continues the process of teaching unique perception. It forces students to see a person and is a good two-person writing activity.

Process: Have each student select a partner and write, in recipe form, directions for duplicating that person. Tell them a recipe is divided into two parts, the ingredients and directions for putting them together. Their goal is to capture the personality of their partner. You may want to read them this example.

Le Michael: Shore Version

Ingredients:

short blond hair
2 green eyes
1 smiling mouth
1 strong body
1 pair dirty, torn tennis shoes

Directions:

Comb hair and part in middle; let wind blow it into place. Place eyes in sunshine to get full twinkle effect. Add tennis shoes and mix in 10,000 freckles. Bake at beach during a good surf. Do all this while laughing and you have one Le Michael: Shore Version.

Have students share their recipes orally and discuss them. Have their recipes captured their partner's personality? Were the directions presented in recipe form? What made some recipes more effective than others? Could you have guessed who they were writing about without knowing their partner? Were the titles of the dishes in keeping with the personality?

These are good assignments to display.

Have students write recipes for war, labor disputes, a president, a good novel, a best friend, a perfect day, and other people, things, and ideas.

3. Developing the Tools of the Writer

*T*here is a paradox in teaching writing. Students need to know about transitions and conclusions before they write an essay, but they need to write an essay in order to work on leads and point of emphasis. They need all the skills of writing an essay, and you can't teach all the skills at once. There is no single wholistic lesson that covers "Writing an Essay" in one period. With this contradiction in mind, this book isolates needed skills and works on those skills. The book is sequentially developmental in approach. The writing activities concentrate on one skill at a time and then to utilize that skill to develop a finished essay. An essay can be three sentences, three paragraphs or three pages.

E.B. White said, "Don't write about Man; write about a man." This advice applies to making assignments. Reduce the length, restrain the scope, clarify a narrower focus—make the assignment possible to handle. You are working on developing skills, not creating publishable works.

That does not mean that your assignments become pabulum. "What I Did on My Summer Vacation" is not the goal. Ask students to observe their physical world, the people world, the idea world, and the other worlds that are relevant to them. Your assignment should expand them; it should be a learning experience, not merely a writing activity. Donald Murray entices us, "The assignment should force him to write just a bit beyond himself. He should always be reaching for an unattainable goal. His writing should have more form, clarity, or grace than that which comes easily to him. He should be stretching his intellectual muscles, moving forward so that he says more and says it more effectively than is normal for him." At our school we ask, "Are you drawing the same picture?" By that we mean: Are you being safe, rather than taking a risk—are you growing rather than vegetating? Remember those kids in class who could always draw beautiful horses, but that was all they could draw?

The activities in this unit are divided into the three processes of writing: prewriting, writing, revision. The lessons are designed to move the student from the initial idea to the first sentence through the steps of development to conclusions and to development of style and unity.

While all the information in this unit should be taught in a sequential manner, the writing activities can be adapted to serve purposes other than what are presented here. (Whenever possible, have students write about content they are studying in your class or another class.)

• *Prewriting* •

Prewriting activities are all those tasks that begin the thinking process. While student may be putting pen to paper, the goal is not a finished product, it is getting organized, trying some words, phrases, sentences out to see how they sound. Prewriting activities can be class presentations that provide a stimulus to write. And prewriting can be those more formal activities like clustering, outlining, and worksheets. It is my belief that prewriting activities should never be graded; the final product is of much more concern. The activities in this section focus on more formal prewriting activities as teachers need to develop their own creative thinking prewriting activities for specific longer assignments.

ACTIVITY 22: CLUSTERING

Clustering is aptly named; it is the gathering of ideas. It is a process that provides writers with a visual picture of their ideas. Below are some examples for preview. To some it may appear as a sloppy person's outline—in a sense it is. It allows ideas to be grouped together and organized without the cumbersome worry of the structure of the model. Gabriele Rico, in her wonderful book *Writing the Natural Way*, gives detailed explanations for developing and using the clustering approach. For very visual, right-brained writers this is perhaps the only idea-gathering model that makes sense to them. The book is well worth investigating.

I suggest students learn clustering on large sheets of paper; they are a kind of brain map of their ideas. On this same sheet they can practice leads, transition sentences, and other prewriting activities. The notes are all in one place and visible at one glance. This is much better than suffering through pages of an outline and rough drafts.

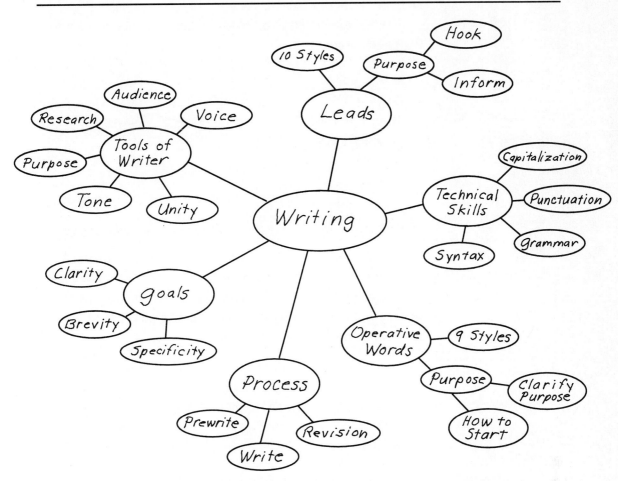

Scope: The purpose of this activity is to introduce the concept of prewriting and have students practice one technique of this process. The activity will take one period. It involves a basic lecture and students working in class on a cluster.

Materials: Large sheets of newsprint or butcher paper.

Process: Explain to students the purpose of prewriting activities as explained in the introduction to this unit.

Brainstorm a list of possible topics for essays that they may be writing this year or are currently working on in class.

Show the students the example of a cluster by photocopying the example from the book or demonstrating it on the board.

Ask students to pick a topic and do a cluster.

You should walk around the room and offer comments as students work on their cluster.

Place these clusters on the walls so students can learn from each other.

~~~~~~~~~~

ACTIVITY 23: OUTLINING

*T*he most important point to teach about outlining is that the outline is for the writer, not for the teacher. Do not get shackled in teaching that all "I's" must have "II's" and all "A's" must have "B's" and so on. The outline should be more like a road map; it should show that you are going from I to IX and that the main stops along the way are II, III and so on. Belaboring *how* to do an outline will result in students never using them.

Scope: The purpose of this activity is to introduce the purpose of outlining and have students learn the process. The activity will take one class period. It involves a presentation by the teacher and students working in class or on a homework assignment

Materials: Either the student's last essay or a photocopied essay from some publication.

Process: Discuss with students the purpose of an outline in aiding writers to get where they are going.

Give students either their last essay or a photocopy of a magazine or newspaper article. Have students outline this writing using the technique of outlining. Have them start several word major heading outlines such as:

I. *Games*
II. *Contact Sports*
III. *Artistic Sports*
IV. *Similarities*
V. *Differences*

Once students have the major headings, have them expand the outline to include the major points of each of the main headings.

I. *Games*
   A. *Historical Background*
   B. *Modern Context*

II. *Contact Sports*
   A. *Football*
   B. *Hockey*

III. *Artistic Sports*
   A. *Gymnastics*
   B. *Diving*

Have students then add supportive points to major points.

I. *Games*
   A. *Historical Background*
      1. *Ancient Games*
      2. *Organized sports in Greece*
      3. *Roman Games*

Students can share their outlines and learn from each other's work.

ACTIVITY 24: GEOMETRIC WRITING (WITH WORKSHEET)

Scope: *T*he purpose of this activity is to present a very structured clustering technique designed to help students organize an essay. The activity involves a teacher presentation and students working in class or as a homework assignment. It will take an entire period.

Materials: Large sheets of newsprint or butcher paper.

Process: Pass out Worksheet 12 and explain the technique and purpose of the geometric worksheet approach to preparing to write an essay. Then pass out the large sheets of paper and help the students fill out the form one step at a time. Explain the forms on the worksheet:

Brainstorm Concept Circle. Ask students to write down different possible topics for an essay. Let their imagination roam—the idea is to get key words, not titles.

Cluster Circle. After some brainstorming ask students to choose one of their ideas. They should place this key word in the middle of the cluster circle and beginning working on key words, ideas, connections from this central idea. It should look like a mini-cluster as in Activity 22.

Focus Triangle. This is where the student gives specific focus to the essay. While the student believes the topic is Russia in the first blank, it may end up being "The Effect of Rasputin on the Royal Family" in the last trapezoid. This helps writers know where they are going.

Parameters Rectangle. This helps writers know how they are going to get where they are going. The operative word should be placed in the center of the rectangle. (A detailed discussion on operative words is in Activity 41.) Writers must decide if they are comparing, discussing, defining, illustrating, or whatever. The operative word defines the approach to be taken.

The top quadrangle is to identify the audience. Is this piece for other students, for a scientific community, a major national magazine, parents—who?

The right quadrangle is to state the piece's purpose. What is the writer attempting to do: convince, inform, enrage, move to action, clarify, present a position—what?

The left quadrangle is to clarify voice/tone. What does this piece sound like: angry, active, lecturing, condescending, moving, warm, hateful—how?

The bottom quadrangle is to state the writer's position in one sentence. Do they place themselves with the administration, the Hemingway fans, the anti-abortionists, the peaceniks, the conservationists, the conservatives, the minimalists, the classicists—where?

For some essays some of the blocks may not be as

relevant as some of the others. That's fine, it is merely a worksheet, not a commitment.

Support Blocks. The top elongated rectangle is for listing the method of development: general to specific, chronological, simple to complex, most important to least important, cause to effect, deductive to inductive—or the reverse of any of these. This will help the student develop a sense of organization for the essay. (See Activity 53.)

The four blocks below the method of development are for support sentences. Students may cite a fact, a personal opinion, an expert opinion, an example, a quote, an analogy. Students need to have done some research to bolster their argument or position.

Style Rectangle. This space is for writing their lead sentence. (Leads are developed extensively in later activities.)

Draft Windows. The first draft window is for a peer to edit the lead. Are there strong nouns and verbs? Does it reflect the stated tone? Is it passive or active? Does it tell or show? Does it grab? Does it inform? Does it work?

The second window is to revise the lead sentence.

The third draft window is to make a mini-outline.

The fourth draft window is for teacher/peers review of the rough draft.

The Geometric Worksheet becomes a valuable blueprint for the essay. It is a constant visual reminder of what should and should not belong in the work.

ACTIVITY 25: POLITICAL ISSUE ESSAY

Students' blank pages do not indicate blank minds. Generally, students don't quite know where they are going with an essay and just can't begin. Prewriting activities help pull good ideas from minds to the page. A worksheet with a few basic, developmental questions can help students determine the direction of their essay.

Scope: This activity will teach students a technique of prewriting for an essay on a political issue. The activity involves a teacher presentation, modeling, in-class writing, and a homework assignment. It will take two class periods.

Process: Explain to students that different types of assignments have different purposes and thus different approaches and style of writing.

I like to approach these types of assignments with a nonsensical one first. It allows students to focus on the process and not what they are going to write: A couple of assignments that have been effective are: "Why ladybug hunting should be stopped in city-funded urban parks" or "Explain the economic and cultural impact of the seaweed shortage on citizens in North Dakota."

Choose one of these nonsensical topics (or one of your own) and have students orally respond to the following points while you write their responses on the board.

1. *What is the topic?* (seaweed shortage)

2. *What is the issue?* (the economic slide of North Dakota as a result of the seaweed shortage and the possible loss of the annual Seaweed Fair and Exposition)

3. *Define the problem.* (seaweed is not being harvested at the same rate in the Sea of Japan and thus shipments to the North Dakota plant have shrunk considerably)

4. *What is the position?* (changing restrictive maritime laws established by the UN that does not allow for inland shipping of sea products)

5. *What is the support?* (Dr. Yuki Tsumi, an expert in seaweed botany has stated, ". . . ."

After students have been through this nonsensical approach, they should understand the format. Now go through it again with a more relevant topic.

Brainstorm with the class a list of current political issues. Have students pick a topic and as they watch you model the process they can create a similar sheet dealing with the topic of their own choice.

Have students complete this form:

Political Issue

1. *What is the topic?* (Endangered species)

2. *What is the issue?* (Saving the environment of the grizzly bear)

3. *Define the problem.* (Every year thousands of acres are being developed, or opened up to tourists that have previously been grizzly wilderness areas.)

4. *What is the position?* (In favor of setting aside additional acreage through federal legislation that will be guaranteed grizzly wilderness areas)

5. *What is the support?* (Dr. Craighead, an internationally recognized expert on the grizzly states, ". . . .")

ACTIVITY 26: ANALYSIS ESSAY

Scope: This activity is designed along the lines of Activity 24 and teaches students another prewriting activity for preparing to write an analytical essay. The activity involves teacher presentation, modeling, and in-class writing. It will take most of the period.

Process: Discuss with students the difference between a fact and an opinion.

Have students complete their own worksheet as you model on the board.

Analysis Essay

1. *Fact:* (Cigarette smoking impairs natural development of the fetus.)

2. *Interpretation:* (More education should be done to convince young women not to take up smoking.)

   or . . . (Women should stop smoking when they become pregnant.)

or . . . (Women who smoke while pregnant should be arrested for child abuse.)

3. *Supporting Evidence:* (Dr. Garcia of the Cancer Institute states, ". . . ."; the Surgeon General of the United States published a report in 1992 entitled "The Myth, The Reality of Smoking" in which it is stated, ". . . ."; the World Book shows the number of new smokers as. . . .)

4. *Options:* (Here the student develops a list of possible options available to addressing their interpretation of the issue.)

This approach will help students realize what research they need to do as a result of deciding what their purpose and direction is going to be.

ACTIVITY 27: BIOGRAPHY ESSAY

Scope: *T*he purpose of this activity is to provide students with an organizational tool when writing biography essays. The activity involves teacher presentation, modeling, and student in-class writing. It will take most of the period and can involve follow-up homework assignments.

Process: Have students fill out their own worksheet as you model on the board.

Biography

1. *Who:* (Mozart)

2. *Where Lived:* (Vienna)

3. *Born/Died:* (1756–91)

4. *Position:* (Mozart was the world's greatest composer.)

5. *Achievements:* (Mozart composed numerous concertos, *operas, symphonies, quartets, and masses.*)

6. *Effect of Achievements:* (Mozart became the standard by which all future composers measured themselves, a rich literature was left for musicians, enriched people's lives.)

7. *Evidence:* (Cite number of pieces written in each category, utilize quote from music expert.)

Discuss the value of this type of prewriting activity for preparing to do a biographical essay.

ACTIVITY 28: GENERAL ESSAY

Scope: This activity will provide students with a prewriting technique for organizing most any general essay. It involves teacher presentation, modeling, and student in-class writing. It will take about half the period.

Process: Have students write on their own paper as you model the following technique on the board.

Have students identify a topic and then fill in the appropriate information for each category.

General Essay

1. *Audience:* (Reading public)

2. *Purpose of essay:* (In a quarter page the student explains the purpose of the essay.)

3. *Style of essay:* (In a half page the student explains the tone, approach, and point of view of the essay.)

4. *Method of Development:* (Most important to least)

5. *Lead:* (Why are present day authors too often overlooked in high school literature programs?)

6. *Area of focus:* (This essay will focus on three living authors—William Kennedy, Jim Carroll, and Jerzy Kosinski—and the value of studying these authors in a high school literature program.)

7. *Supporting Evidence: (*Get personal opinions from students, quotes from educational journals and reviews of these authors' works.)

ACTIVITY 29: ARGUMENTATION ESSAY

Scope: The purpose of this activity is to provide students with another worksheet model that can be used as a prewriting organizational technique when preparing an essay of argumentation. It involves teacher presentation, modeling, and student in-class writing. It will take most of the period.

Process: Have students fill out a sheet of their own as you model this approach on the board.

Argumentation

1. *Debate Topic:* (Resolved: The United States should maintain a military and diplomatic position that maintains freedom of passage in the Persian Gulf.)

2. *Pro Position:* (Those in favor are concerned with the maritime tradition of equal access of all nations to international waters.)

3. *Con Position:* (Those opposed feel that the U.S. is putting itself in a vulnerable position both militarily and politically by taking such an aggressive stance over a minor issue.)

4. *Supporting Evidence Pro:* (List of information the Pro side will use)

5. *Supporting Evidence Con:* (List of information the Con side will use)

6. *My position:* (Statement of personal position on issue)

• *Writing* •

The activities in this section deal with eleven ingredients of the writing process: leads, transitions, supportive sentences, conclusions, operative words, unity, methods of development, style, tone, showing, and point of view. It is more effective to isolate each of these functions and teach it than it is to assign essays and then criticize students for not using these techniques appropriately.

When asked who the greatest writer was, one man responded, "The guy who wrote Dodgers on the Brooklyn uniforms. Look at that royal blue on the grey background, the sweeps and curls of those letters. It's something isn't?" In a way he was right; certainly it has style, impact and creates an image. That writer was effective. Your students can be effective too by sequentially going through each of these techniques and then eventually putting each step together to create the successful essay.

ACTIVITY 30: INTRODUCING THE LEAD

*M*ost of the time that students say they spend writing, they actually spend sitting, staring, moaning, doodling, and finally quitting. This is the time before the first sentence goes on the page. What they need to learn is how to write a lead. I remember listening to an author tell a television host that what she wrote best was her autograph. She knew how to start, where she was going and when to stop, and she could spell it. Having command of different styles of leads can render that first essay sentence as easy as the autograph.

Scope: The purpose of this activity is to introduce students to the concept that the purpose of the lead is to HOOK the readers and to INFORM them. It will teach students some specific styles of leads. It will take about four or five class periods. It involves teacher presentation, oral writing, in-class writing, and homework assignments.

Process: Students will need to take detailed notes during this presentation.

Give students the name of the lead (see below), its definition, and an example. Then give them a topic and ask them to provide an oral lead. Elicit as many oral leads as you feel you need for the students to understand the concept before moving to the next one. Format, not style, is the point. Use this same approach for each lead.

Thesis Restatement. This is the most commonly used lead. If the assignment is, "Describe the most notorious character you have ever met," the lead restates the question into a statement: "The most notorious character I ever met was my maternal grandmother Erin who smoked long cigars and drank gin."

Informational. This is also a commonly taught lead. It calls for telling the reader exactly what is the purpose of the paper. "The purpose of this paper is to examine the five causes of the Civil War," or "This paper examines the character development of Romeo and Juliet in William Shakespeare's classic play," or "The dark side and the bright side of artist Vincent Van Gogh are presented in this essay." Informational, but not great hooks.

Question. Marshall McLuhan would label the question a hot medium. You cannot ask a question without the reader subconsciously answering it—thus the reader is engaged. "Have you just wished you climbed a mountain, floated the Colorado, jumped out of a plane—or are you really willing to do it?"

One Word. The one-word lead is powerful and should be used selectively. Find the major concept of your essay and choose an emotional word that represents it. State the word as a single sentence and then follow that sentence with one of explanation. "Terror. This is the only word to describe how Jenny Hawes felt as the shark inched its way toward her," or "Guts. Jimmy Conners proved he had lots of them when he went five sets to win the Wimbeldon Championship in 100-

degree heat against a much younger player." What doesn't work is a weak word that offers no impact. "Clothes. I have lots of them in my closet."

Quotation. This is particularly effective in students' work. It gives the essay immediate authority. "It is clear that the NASA digital component is far superior to the Russian-made model," stated Noble Prize winner in Physics, Olaf Svendenson.

The format of the quotation can come in three styles: all the quote and then the source; the source and then all the quote; or half the quote, the source, and the rest of the quote.

Congressional Document #45 states, "The men of the Veracruz had no chance to escape."

"I will never write a work as powerful as Being There," stated Jerzy Kosinski, "but I may write a better one."

"This is a sad day for the dance world. We have lost one of our greatest—Fred Astaire," eulogized Gene Kelly.

Also keep in mind that quotes are not merely what people say, but what information is taken from another source—Time magazine reported, "Over 50,000 stock brokers have been investigated for possible fraud in the last two years."

Flashback. This is a great hook but a little tricky for students to get hold of at first. It takes a situation in the present and reflects on an event in the past which is analogous.

As the bodies return home from El Salvador I could not help remembering those flag-draped coffins postmarked Vietnam.

The smell in the kitchen immediately took me back to the first time I smelled pumpkin soup, at my grandmother's when I was five.

Fireworks were painting the sky, the band filled the air waves and patriotism grabbed each parade viewer as a similar parade must have 100 years earlier at the Centennial Celebration of the Constitution.

Thrust. "Blood was dripping down my face and Paul was nowhere to be seen. Why had I agreed to a gang fight?" Make you feel like you came in the middle of a story? That is a thrust lead. It is a popular approach in television shows. It puts you five minutes into the story and then gradually takes you back to the beginning. While the first sentence is a great hook, the following sentences have to be strong on information in order to clarify the topic of the essay for the reader.

Fiction/fact. This lead starts out as if it might be a story (fiction) but then comes full circle to the real subject of the essay. "Ernest cast the fly onto the placid stream and instantly the rainbow devoured the morsel as if in rage; this was the kind of day Ernest Hemingway liked to have when relaxing from the pressures of writing in Sun Valley, Idaho."

Journalism. This is the backbone of leads. The journalism lead gives the reader the who, what, why, where, when and how of a story. The 5 W's and an H. Not all essays warrant all six, but the approach is useful. "The *Federalist Papers*, written through collaboration by Alexander Hamilton and James Madison in 1787, was designed to influence the Americans to support the new Constitution."

Staccato. Your music majors will identify with this: short and repetitive. The purpose of this style lead is to present a great deal of information all at once. This lead works most effectively with journalism-style stories and description essays. "Green grass . . . red clay . . . a white ball. These are less observed colors of the national pastime's opening day."

You can usually teach about four leads a day. At the end of each day, have students write one of each of the leads on an assigned topic and one of each of the leads on four different topics. Thus they have four leads on one subject and four leads on four different subjects.

When students come to class the next day, orally share their leads and have the class comment. Then address the next four leads the same way as you did with the first four and make the same homework assignment.

Once you have completed this process with all ten leads, pass out Worksheet 13 and have students review the leads.

You will find you have to review leads; do not rush this activity—it is critical to the later success of your program. After you have reviewed the worksheet, have students write one example of each lead on the same subject and one example of each lead on different subjects.

Next comes the first of two quizzes. The first one is Worksheet 14 with nine leads and the students are to identify the style of each. This should be corrected orally so that students can discuss and debate their choices.

The second quiz is Worksheet 15 and asks students to write a lead on a specific subject for each on a single sheet.

Spend a great deal of time editing the results of Worksheet 15. Pass back the worksheet to be rewritten.

Finally, ask students to write ten leads, one of each style on an assigned topic, one of each style on any topic they chose. This gives them some understanding that not all topics are geared for each style of lead. Fitting the lead to the topic becomes critical as students develop their writing skills.

The last day on this activity, students can share in class what they feel is their best lead. Ask students to develop that lead into a three-paragraph essay.

ACTIVITY 31: TRANSITIONS BY WORD

*T*he purpose of the transition sentence is to move the reader smoothly from one paragraph to another. In order for the essay to have unity the reader needs to see a relationship between each succeeding paragraph. The way to work on transitions is not to assign essays and then correct the four or five transition sentences. It is better to isolate that goal and work on it exclusively and then have students incorporate this skill into their other writing.

A consistent use of transitions can be the recurring thread that ties the piece together. Constant referral without being overly repetitious can provide the reader with constant connections and review.

Scope: The purpose of this activity is to introduce the concept of transitions and develop the technique of transition by word. The activity should take half a class period. It involves teacher presentation and students' oral writing.

Process: Explain to students that the purpose of a transition is to smoothly move from one paragraph to another and thus establish the relationship between the topics of the first paragraph and the related topic of the second paragraph.

Have students develop a list of transition words. Using a transition word or phrase is the easiest approach to writing a transition sentence.

The list may include:

additionally, admittedly, also, although, and, as assuredly, besides, but, certainly, clearly, consequently, even so, finally, first, (second, third, etc.) for, furthermore, for example, for instance, granted, hence, however, if, in addition, in fact, indeed, it's true that, moreover, needless to say, nevertheless, next, no doubt, nobody denies, nor, obviously, of course, on the other hand, or, rather, since, so, still, the fact remains that, then, therefore, thus, to be sure, undoubtedly, unless, whether, while, and yet.

Give students some sentences orally as if they were the topic sentence of a paragraph; then call on students to give the transition sentence.

Ten minutes of this oral work is much more effective than assigning an essay and correcting the transition sentences. It also allows students to focus on one skill and vary their approach, take risks, experiment with language and structure.

ACTIVITY 32: TRANSITION BY STYLE

Scope: The purpose of this activity is to teach students a second type of transition technique. The activity involves teacher presentation and oral writing on the part of students. Allow a full period for this activity.

Process: Present to students the following material on divergent types of transition sentences. After presenting a type and giving an example, present the students with the topic of a first paragraph and the related topic of a second paragraph and ask them to give the transition sentence. Use as many examples as you need so that the students demonstrate an understanding of the concept.

Transition by Steps. These transitions move us sequentially from the first step to the final step.

Following the mental preparation needed to play in the Super Bowl the players must arrive at the stadium hours before the game to prepare their bodies.

It is clear that the first paragraph must have dealt with the mental preparation of the players for the game. The second paragraph is going to address the process that players go through in the locker room before the game, such as whirlpools, taping, and massage. Notice that the words *prepare/preparation* are used to suggest a connection between the two paragraphs' ideas.

Transition by Example. The purpose here is to give an example that will move the essay forward, making a connection between paragraph one and paragraph two.

While racism exists everywhere in the world, only The Republic of South Africa embraces it as an official governmental policy.

The first paragraph must have dealt with the large concept of general racism, and the second paragraph will examine the specific racist policies of South Africa.

Transition by Result. This is a cause-and-effect style transition. It helps students draw conclusions as they write.

But the Nobel Prize for Literature was not the only result of John Steinbeck's writing; he also touched the lives of millions of American high school students who studied his novels.

While the first paragraph must have been a review of Steinbeck's life and his awards, the next paragraph will be more personal and will deal with the actual impact of his writing.

Transition by Repetition. While most teachers are concerned about students reusing words in their essays, it is a valuable style of transition if used sparingly. Let the entire sentence do the job rather than a standard transition word. Does the last sentence of the previous paragraph provide a word, a phrase, or an idea that could be the basis of the transition sentence in the next paragraph? The format of this technique is to repeat key base words in order to show connection.

When the dust had finally cleared it was the two warriors who faced each other alone.
They were warriors from hell—criminals from the ghetto with nothing to lose and perhaps nothing to gain because this fight between their two gangs would not better their lives.

This transition repeats the war concept, indicating that paragraph one must have set the physical scene and paragraph two the emotional or personal scene

ACTIVITY 33: TRANSITION THROUGH PARALLEL CONSTRUCTION

Scope: The purpose of this activity is to teach a third style of transition sentences to be used to create parallel construction between paragraphs. It is similar in approach to the two previous activities involving presentation and oral writing. It will take most of a class period. This is the most difficult of all the transition styles, and you may wish to teach it only to the most advanced classes.

Process: Present to students the pairs of words or phrases below which are called "balanced connectives." Have students write them down. After you have given them a pair, ask a student to write a transition sentence using the approach.

as . . . as
both . . . and
either . . . or

neither . . . nor
not only . . . but also
on the one hand . . . on the other hand
just as . . . so too
in general . . . in particular
on the one side . . . on the other
in that case . . . but in this case
While . . . conversely
Though . . . never (always, sometimes, rarely, usually)

ACTIVITY 34: ISOLATED PRACTICE ON THE TRANSITION

Scope: This activity gives students the opportunity to work with all the transition styles at once without having to be concerned with writing an essay. When first reading this activity, teachers sometimes think it is silly—in fact it is one of the most successful teaching activities in the book. Students like to refer to this activity as the "Blah, Blah, Blah Assignment."

The activity involves giving students directions, doing some modeling on the board, and finally giving a homework assignment.

Process: Write a lead sentence on the board. Then underneath, on the next three lines, write *blah, blah, blah*. Then ask students to come up with a transition sentence to the next paragraph. Remember the transition can either be the last line of the first paragraph or the first line of the second paragraph. Continue with this process until you have a full essay "written."

Assign students to go through the same process as homework. Fifteen transition sentences are not too large an assignment. You may want to share the following example with students so that they more clearly understand the directions of the assignment.

Junk. Food, not leftover alarm clocks, broken chairs, and worn out tennis shoes.

blah blah blah (Students literally write "blah blah blah" in place of a full paragraph.)

But poor health is only one of the results of eating too much junk food.

blah blah blah

Eating lots of foods with preservatives, artificial flavors, and injected hormones will result in poor mental performance.

blah blah blah

Not only will poor intellectual growth be a result of poor eating habits, but also one needs to consider their physical appearance.

blah blah blah

Therefore, by following these four simple rules, you can eat well and eat cheaply in order to achieve a healthy body and a healthy mind.

When you collect this assignment make sure that students don't merely write an essay and insert *blah, blah, blah* between sentences as in the example below.

Do you like junk food?
blah blah blah
I really like to eat it.
blah blah blah
The reason I like it is because it is quick.
blah blah blah
And inexpensive also.

The purpose of transitions, and of this activity, is to move from one idea to the next smoothly and clearly, not to write a paragraph with *blah, blah, blah* in the middle. Thus you may want to do this assignment again until they have mastered all three styles of transition writing.

ACTIVITY 35: INTRODUCING SUPPORTIVE SENTENCES

Scope: *S*upportive sentences are the building blocks of a quality paper. This activity will introduce students to ways of using them. The activity involves teacher presentation and oral writing. It should take half the period.

Materials: Bag with assorted objects in it.

Process: Explain to students that supportive sentences provide the information supporting the writer's central thesis.

Identify and define for the students each of the different styles of supportive sentences: **quotations** involve not only what a person says, but what another source has written; **facts** are generally accepted pieces of information; **opinions** are either personal or expert (while the author's attitude about some subjects may be important, an expert opinion often gives the essay more punch, more authority); **examples** are sentences that provide illustrations of the point being made; **analogies** are sentences that cite circumstances or outcomes similar to the one being discussed in the paper.

Discuss with the students the difference between observations and conclusions. Have a student reach into a bag and, without looking, make observations. Very often the student merely responds, "It is a hair brush." That is a conclusion, not an observation. An observation would be, "It is about six inches long; it appears to be made of plastic; one side is bristly and the other smooth." It is typical for students to use conclusions instead of observations in their writing. A student may give the entire cause and effect of World War II without any evidence building. It is important for students to draw small conclusions from large amounts of evidence rather than the reverse.

You may want to assign students to write one sentence that is an observation and one sentence that is a conclusion on the same subject.

ACTIVITY 36: PRACTICING SUPPORTIVE SENTENCES

Scope: *T*he purpose of this activity is to expand on the concept of observation and conclusion by addressing the topics of fact and opinion. The activity involves teacher presentation, oral writing, and possible homework assignments. It should take half a class period.

Process: Ask students the following questions:

Can you prove "Raiders of the Lost Ark" was the best motion picture?

Can you prove "Raiders of the Lost Ark" grossed more money than any other film?

Can you prove "Raiders of the Lost Ark" won more awards than any other film?

Can you prove "Raiders of the Lost Ark" was the most well-liked film by people under 25?

If all of the above are true, can you prove "Raiders of the Lost Ark" was the best motion picture?

Can you prove that Miss Indiana was the most beautiful girl in the United States in 1988?

Can you prove that the judges of the Miss America pageant thought Miss Indiana was the most beautiful girl in the 1988 pageant?

Give students some questions that they turn from fact to opinion or opinion into fact. E.g.:

Bob is the smartest student at UC Berkeley.
Bob has the highest SAT scores at UC Berkeley.

Ernie Banks is the greatest baseball player of all time.
Ernie Banks was a 12 year All Star for the Chicago Cubs, was twice chosen Most Valuable Player, and ended his career with a .303 lifetime batting average.

Continue with examples until students understand the concept. You may want to assign this activity as a homework assignment or move on to the next activity.

ACTIVITY 37: TYING SUPPORTIVE SENTENCES TO LEADS

Scope: This activity is designed to allow students to utilize what they have learned about supportive sentences and practice leads at the same time. It involves about 5–10 minutes of directions and homework.

Process: Have students write a good strong lead. Then they are to write an example of each type of supporting sentence that could be used in an essay

As in the previous activities, students should not worry about accuracy: the idea is to learn the format. Thus students can just invent the information. The goal is to work on supportive sentences, not research skills. Share these orally next class to make sure everyone is clear on how to use supportive sentences.

ACTIVITY 38: PROVIDING THE MISSING CONCLUSION PARAGRAPH

The most common mistake in conclusions is that they often have little to do with the lead of the essay. The conclusion is not the time for new information. If it wasn't in the body of the essay it does not belong in the conclusion. The conclusion is where the essay gets tidied up. The strings are pulled together, there is a summary of the main points, and the author makes the final punch statement. In format the conclusions should merely be a deepening of the lead statement. It is a justification; it should tell what was presented and why. The final sentence can be a quote, a personal statement by the writer, a prediction, a brief summary, an inference based upon the final event of the essay, an analogy, a revision or a repeat of the lead. But most importantly the conclusion of a piece of writing is not simply writing "The End."

Scope: The purpose of this activity is to teach students the goals of conclusion and to let them practice writing them. It involves teacher presentation and either in-class writing or homework.

Materials: Photocopied articles.

Process: Give students copies of short newspaper or magazine articles; the Op-Ed page is a good source, but omit the final paragraphs.

Have students develop the concluding statements themselves, then compare their work with the original conclusions.

Discuss with the class: Is the conclusion based on the topic sentence and paragraph? Does it support evidence presented in the body of the paper? Was new information brought out in the conclusion that was not identified in the body of the paper? Did the conclusion hold together based upon the material discussed? Did it have a final punch?

ACTIVITY 39: REVISING THE WRITERS' CONCLUSIONS

Scope: This activity will bring even more clarity to writing conclusions. It involves teacher directions and in-class writing or homework.

Materials: Photocopies of famous speeches such as John Kennedy's Inaugural Address, Christ's Sermon on the Mount, Lincoln's Gettysburg Address, Churchill's Battle of Britain speech, Martin Luther King's "I Have a Dream" speech, omitting the final paragraph.

Process: After students have heard or read the speech, have them write the final paragraph, trying to maintain the style and content of the original. Emphasize to students that conclusions stem from evidence presented in the main body of the essay.

ACTIVITY 40: DRAWING CONCLUSIONS

Scope: This activity is an entertaining way to present the idea that a conclusion should be written based upon the evidence presented. It involves teacher presentation and students writing in class. It should take about half the period.

Process: Read to student the following list of statements and ask them to write a conclusion paragraph.

1. *There have been five murders on Elm Street.*

2. *The street has only one street light.*

3. *One end of the street is alongside the river bank where gangs hang out.*

4. *Walking down Elm Street will cut 20 minutes off my walk home.*

It is fun to have students write concluding statements after hearing each piece of information and then seeing how their conclusions change as they learn more information.

ACTIVITY 41: INTRODUCING OPERATIVE WORDS

Operative words are the key words of an assignment; they specify to the writer exactly what should be done in the essay and focus the approach to be used. An essay to compare is going to have a different format, with a different objective, than an essay to describe. One of the most common faults of young writers is that they do not answer the question asked in an assignment or on a test.

Scope: The purpose of this activity is to introduce students to operative words so that they can learn what they are and how they direct the development of an essay.

The format for teaching operative words is identical to teaching leads in Activity 30 and includes teacher presentation and oral writing, as well as homework. This activity will take three to four class periods.

Process: Give students an overview of all nine operative words by presenting the operative word, defining it, giving an example, and then asking students to orally write examples.

Summarize. An assignment to summarize asks students to give the main points of anything they have read, or in brief form restate the main events or steps of something. Skill in summarizing would allow students to write an essay on: *Summarize the budget cuts proposed by President Reagan in 1988.*

Prove. An assignment to prove asks students to give factual information to show why something is true. Skill in summarizing would allow students to write an essay on: *Prove that Shakespeare did in fact live in Stratford-Upon-Avon and was a playwright.*

Illustrate. An assignment to illustrate asks students to give examples to support a central thesis. Skill in illustration would allow students to write an essay on: *Illustrate the inhumanity of the American government toward Native Americans in the 1890s.*

Describe. An assignment to describe asks students to use their senses to give the reader the same experience they had, by showing. Skill in description would allow students to write an essay on: *Describe the character Chance in* Being There.

Explain. An assignment to explain asks students to tell how or why something happened or works. Skill in explaining would allow students to write an essay on: *Explain how Michelangelo painted the Sistine Chapel.*

Define. An assignment to explain asks students to give the exact meaning of something and show how it is different from something similar. Skill in defining would allow students to write an essay on: *Define Hemingway's concept of manhood as shown in* The Old Man and the Sea.

Compare/contrast. An assignment to compare also asks students to contrast, to show the similarities and differences. Skill in comparing and contrasting would allow students to write an essay on: *Compare Teddy Roosevelt's view of the Latin American world with that of Franklin Roosevelt.*

Evaluate. An assignment to evaluate asks students to make a judgment based upon internal and external evidence. Skill in evaluating would allow students to write an essay on: *Evaluate the value of a high school literature program as a part of students' lifelong goals.*

Synthesize/analyze. Students have great difficulty getting a handle on these two words. An assignment to synthesize asks students to put parts together to explain a whole; to analyze asks to explain a whole based upon the parts. The process is the same, only the direction is different. Skill in analyzing or synthesizing would allow students to write an essay on: *Analyze the functioning of a car.* (In one case the writer would talk about the overall purpose and makeup of a car and then deal with each of the individual systems. With the other approach, the author would first take each system of the car in some sequential order and then tell about the overall functioning of the car.)

ACTIVITY 42: THE RIGHT OPERATIVE WORDS TELL YOU WHAT TO WRITE

Scope: This activity is a simple oral test of the students' knowledge of operative words. It will give you an idea of what material needs to be reviewed. Oral questioning by the teacher and oral or written responses by the students are required. The activity should take one period.

Process: Make up writing assignments for each of the operative words. (Students might enjoy making up some of these assignments.) Ask students what they would do if they were given one of these assignments. This will show whether they clearly know what each operative word asks them to do.

Finally, read some leads to the students and ask them what the operative word must have been in the assignment. This will help students make a connection between what they write as the lead and what the assignment asked them to do.

ACTIVITY 43: TESTING YOUR OPERATIVE WORD IQ

Scope: *T*his activity involves three operative word tests that will help students and teacher determine what material needs to reviewed before moving on to other activities. Remember the tests are to be a learning experience more than an evaluative tool.

This activity involves about five minutes of directions for each test and students can complete a test in half a period. Do not give both tests on the same day.

Process: Hand out Worksheet 16 and ask students to complete and hand in. Follow the same process for Worksheets 17 and 18.

ACTIVITY 44: CREATING ASSIGNMENTS WITH OPERATIVE WORDS

Scope: *T*his activity helps students learn about operative words by taking on the teacher role. It involves five minutes of directions and either in-class or homework writing.

Process: Ask students to write one sentence assignments using each of the operative words.

Very often I take the most creative assignment for each word and use it as a class assignment.

ACTIVITY 45: NINE ASSIGNMENTS FOR NINE OPERATIVE WORDS

Scope: *T*he purpose of this activity is to make students conscious of using the proper lead with the right operative word and learn that not all leads work with all assignments. It will give students further practice on learning and using operative words.

The activity involves oral presentation of directions and writing in class or as homework. It will take 6 or 7 class periods.

These writing assignments are designed to be only a half page of writing, certainly no more than a page. Students are still working on all the writing skills that have been learned to date. Later you can worry about final products. Now is the chance for you to work on creative/ambiguous assignments. You may want to adapt some of the assignments in Unit 4 for these assignments.

Process: Each class period, review two operative words and give students two half-page assignments based upon the suggested assignments below. (They are much more effective when you can integrate writing assignments with the literature they are reading or the social science they are studying. Whenever possible, use writing assignments that make connections with content areas.)

The next class period, share what students have written and do some form of discussion and evaluation.

Compare/contrast: In a short essay, compare and contrast two emotions. In a second short essay, compare and contrast two physical objects.

Describe: Wash your hands with salt and just a tablespoon of water, rinse your hands thoroughly and then rub in some lotion. Describe this activity.

Evaluate: Evaluate what would be the most effective kind of punishment for you and for the class.

Summarize: Summarize the main reasons that grumpfs are becoming more and more disliked in Togandoland.

Explain: Explain what you would see if you rode through space on the front of a beam of light.

Synthesize/analyze: Synthesize the workings of your latest successful invention that 3M or General Electric has agreed to manufacture.

Define: Look up a word in the dictionary that you have never encountered before; write an essay defining the word.

Illustrate: Ladybug hunting is quite controversial in the Northwest. Illustrate people's attitudes and feelings toward this practice.

Prove: Take something that is untrue and write an essay proving it is.

ACTIVITY 46: USING ALL THE OPERATIVE WORDS IN ONE ASSIGNMENT

Scope: This activity is designed to teach students how all the operative words are related together in a writing assignment. It involves five minutes of oral directions and writing at home or in class.

Process: The final activity on operative words begins with a discussion with students. It demonstrates that as they learn more about writing and operative words, they will be using more than one operative word in an assignment. When students are asked to describe the day at the beach, they also may get into defining joy and proving that sun rays can cause pain. Ask students to work up an assignment that realistically uses as many operative words as possible. The task is to create an assignment, not to write an essay. For example:

Define *communism and* compare *it to socialism.* Evaluate *the effectiveness of communism in Russia and* describe *how the* peasants function under this system. Summarize *the main points of Lenin's revolutionary declaration and* explain *how it led to the revolution in 1917*. Analyze *the workings of the present communist structure giving illustrations of its successes and* prove *that the economics of supply and demand have no bearing in the communist economy.*

ACTIVITY 47: TYING OPERATIVE WORDS TO LEADS

Scope: *I*t is important to work specifically on how operative words are tied to leads. This and the next writing strategies are designed for that purpose.

This assignment involves giving five minutes of directions each class period, allowing time for students to write in class, and then assigning homework.

Process: Give students these directions:

Write an assignment for each of the operative words. Underline the operative word in each assignment. Next determine the style of lead you feel would best compliment that assignment. Finally write the lead for the assignment. Use each style of lead.

A paper would look like this:

Write an essay that describes *your feelings when alone. Staccato: "Fear . . . unsure . . . lost. These are some of the feelings I have when I am left alone at night."*

Students would follow the above format for each of the operative words. Students must have at least one of each kind of lead.

ACTIVITY 48: TYING OPERATIVE WORDS, LEADS, AND TRANSITIONS

Scope: *T*his writing activity is designed for students to begin to pull the strings together of all the techniques taught so far. It involves giving directions in class and either making homework assignments or providing class time to write.

Process: Students are given an assignment for each of the operative words. Next they choose a different lead for each assignment. They are then to write the lead. Following the lead they are to use one of the transition techniques and write a transition sentence. The final sentence should be a conclusion style sentence. Thus they will have written a three-sentence essay.

Below is an example of how the paper would look:

Evaluate whether you could have kissed John Merrick as Mrs. Kendall did in the film "The Elephant Man."

Question Lead: *Is it possible to see beauty, sensitivity and intelligence inside a deformed, tumor ridden body? Clearly* (transition by word) *Mrs. Kendall did, as she gave John Merrick the only gift she could, a sense that he was normal. In reviewing this scene I doubt whether I would have the courage and compassion of Mrs. Kendall.*

ACTIVITY 49: INTRODUCING UNITY OF AN ESSAY

Scope: *T*he purpose of this activity is to provide material to present to students on the concept of unity in writing. It involves an oral presentation by you, as well as leading a discussion and students filling out Worksheet 19.

Process: Pass out to students the worksheet and have them take notes as you present the following material.

Unity of Subject. Simply put, this is writing about what you said you were going to write about.

Unity of Scope. Each of the main points should be treated with the same depth and volume of information.

Unity of Tone. Tone provides the "feel" of the author for the subject. Poe's choice of words clearly gives students the sense of impending darkness, dampness, terror. When writing nonfiction, an author should have a tone which is clear and unaffected. Most important, it should remain constant throughout the piece. The choice of words is what gives tone; they should be appropriate to the task and fit in with the words surrounding them. Students should also keep in mind the concept of showing and not telling. A misplaced word, phrase, or sentence sticks out like a wilted daisy in a basket of long stem roses—it doesn't fit. Students often use a single ten-dollar word in a one-dollar essay, or throw in some slang in a formal essay, or use some profanity not for emphasis but for effect. The piece is either all classical, all rock, all country, or all blues. But the tone must remain consistent.

Unity of Style. Like tone, you should keep to one style. Style is how you, and why you, put words together. If the piece is to be a sensitive portrayal of my feelings for my mom, throwing in some off-color jokes about women would not fit; if the essay is an offhanded look at school, a deep philosophical discussion on the nature of learning would be out of place. It must be clear that the same author, with the same objective, wrote the entire work. If you were reading a description of the ocean by John Steinbeck, would you notice if I slipped in a sentence from Poe on the sea? (Not only would the "sound" be different, but one other difference would be that Steinbeck would call it the ocean and Poe the sea.)

Unity of Point-of-View. Who is telling the story or writing the essay and in what tense must remain consistent throughout the piece.

Discuss with the class how tone and emphasis are created in daily conversation: sound of the voice, gestures, facial expression, inflection.

Ask the students how to create it in written work: amount of space provided for certain points, repetition, choice of words, placement on the page, attitude of author toward the subject.

Next discuss how tone and emphasis are not created effectively: superficial use of exclamation points ("He is a good player!"); weak use of passive voice ("The ball was hit by the bat"—give other oral examples and have students change from passive to active); use of vague rather than concrete terms ("At that point in time"); euphemisms ("Japanese relocation centers" instead of "concentration camps", or "individuals maintaining an inconsistent income" rather than "unemployed"); worn-out words (your students will tell you the current buzz words and phrases); clichés ("nothing ventured, nothing gained"); hyperbole ("I've told you a million times"); intensives used for emphasis when in fact their banality de-emphasizes ("That was a really interesting movie" or "That girl is so cute").

Have students give oral examples for each of these blocks to creating tone and emphasis. Finally, list these few technical tips for development of solid style.

1. *Don't overuse the verb "to be."*

2. *Vary sentence length.*

3. *Vary sentence structure. Use simple, compound, complex, and compound-complex sentences.*

4. *Write about what you care.*

5. *Get to it—don't ramble.*

6. *Simple, direct declarative sentences often are the strongest ones.*

7. *Write standard English—not slang, not Elizabethan, and not something else.*

8. *Communicate—there is a real person reading your work. Say what you mean to say.*

9. *Before you write, have something to say.*

ACTIVITY 50: MOST CRITICAL TOOL OF WRITING: THE EAR

Scope: The purpose of this activity is to train the ear as an effective editing and writing tool. It involves teaching reading to the students and then having a discussion about the concept of unity of tone and style. It takes one class period to complete.

Process: Have students listen to a number of essays on the same topic and then compare the different styles, points-of-view, and tone. Theodore Cheney (in *Getting the Words Right*) suggests six paragraphs on cabins. (See Appendix B for examples.)

It is also very effective to use some of your favorite literature on the same topic. Particularly accessible are character descriptions.

ACTIVITY 51: PRACTICING LACK OF UNITY

Scope: An effective way to learn a skill is to practice it incorrectly. This activity will help train students' ears to recognize lack of unity. It involves oral directions and a 25-minute writing and sharing activity.

Process: Assign the class a topic on which to write a three-sentence paragraph. Have each student write the paragraph, fold the page over so that the paragraph is covered, and pass it to the person on the right. That student writes what would have been the second paragraph of her/his own essay. Then repeat the process for a third paragraph, which should be the concluding paragraph to that student's essay. These essays can then be shared with a discussion on the lack of unity.

ACTIVITY 52: PRACTICING DIFFERENT TONES AND STYLES

Scope: This activity is designed to utilize all the concepts of unity in writing a short essay. It involves a short set of directions and in-class writing or homework.

Process: Have students choose a general topic, such as cabins, and write three essays, each about one long paragraph. Each mini-essay should have a different tone and style.

Be sure you are continually sharing and using the evaluation techniques now that students are beginning to write on a regular basis.

ACTIVITY 53: INTRODUCING METHODS OF ESSAY DEVELOPMENT

Scope: Once students have an idea of WHAT they want to talk about they often don't know HOW to go about it. Presenting information about methods of developing an essay will give students a structure to hang on to while they develop their skills. The activity involves a teacher presentation and takes about half the period.

Process: Present to students the following information on methods of essay development and discuss.

Chronology: *past to present, from first events to last.*

Simple to Complex: *the easiest point to the hardest.*

Spatial: *from right to left, up to down, inside to out.*

General to Specific: *large concept to specific examples.*

Conclusion to Evidence: *from the result to the facts.*

Emphasis: *from least important to most important.*

Cause to Effect: *from origin to outcome.*

All these approaches can be in reversed order. After having presented this material and given sufficient examples, I then throw out a number of topics and ask which of the approaches would be best suited for developing the essay.

ACTIVITY 54: MATCHING OPERATIVE WORDS TO METHODS OF DEVELOPMENT

Scope: This activity will help students understand the relationship between what operative words tell you to do and choosing the best method of essay development to accomplish that goal. It involves a brief set of directions and either class writing time, homework, or oral writing in class.

Process: Students write three examples of essay questions that would be best suited for each of the methods of development presented in the previous exercise.

ACTIVITY 55: UTILIZING MULTIPLE METHODS FOR A SINGLE ESSAY

Scope: This activity is similar in scope to Activity 46; it teaches students how multiple methods of essay development can be used in a single essay. It can be done as a written assignment or orally in class.

Process: Students draft a detailed writing assignment indicating which sections of the assignment would warrant which approach.
For example:

Discuss the events of World War II (chronology), *identify the need for a world organization following that war* (cause and effect), *and evaluate whether the United Nations would be capable of preventing World War III* (evidence to conclusion).

Writing a couple of assignments like this will help students realize that, like leads and operative words, different approaches can be combined in a single essay as long as a consistent structure and focus is maintained.

ACTIVITY 56: INTRODUCING STYLE

*I*n William Strunk and E.B. White's *Elements of Style,* the authors are not referring to how Paula Abdul dresses or how Mrs. Bush conducts a dinner party or how the Reverend Jesse Jackson delivers a speech. They are referring to the technical elements of writing—how words are properly put together. While Strunk/White are certainly in favor of vigorous, active prose, they do not deal with style as I do here until the last section of their book. And in that section they still hedge.

Style is the sense of what is distinguished and distinguishing. Here we leave solid ground. Who can confidently say what ignites a certain combination of words, causing them to explode in the mind. Who knows why certain notes in music are capable of stirring the listener deeply, though the same notes slightly rearranged are impotent....there is no satisfactory explanation of style.

By sixth grade, most students can write grammatically correct sentences, but they can't write speeches like Martin Luther King, Jr. A relatively bright junior high student knows all the words in Hemingway's novels but is not be able to put them together as Hemingway did. Since we can't define style, surely we can't teach it. Right. But you can show students that they should be learning to recognize style and developing their own style. A writer's style is primarily learned by ineffectively copying a favorite author's style until students become good enough writers to realize what terrible copiers they are and begin to develop their own unique use of words. Such copying is to be expected, encouraged, and utilized.

Scope: This activity allows students to try to copy certain styles in order to learn they have to find their own voice. It requires reading some passages to students, and students doing some oral and in-class writing.

Process: Read to the class a few sentences they have all heard and have them revise them. Let them learn that style works and bad style doesn't work.

Here are some examples:

"It was the best of times, it was the worst of times. . . ." (A Tale of Two Cities)

(After attempting to edit that sentence, students generally find they can't improve it. Strunk and White suggest Thomas Paine's "These are the times that try men's souls." They might make it clearer, more specific, but not as powerful.)

John Kennedy's "Ask not what your country can do for you, but ask what you can do for your country." A look at the consistent parallel construction and compare/contrast style of most of Kennedy's speeches is an interesting study in style.

Have students revise "December 7, 1941, a day that will live in infamy," from FDR. (What else needed to be said?)

Use some of your favorite examples. Students begin to see that style is that intangible that makes the written word exciting to read and write.

ACTIVITY 57: STYLE VERSUS FAD

While students can't be taught style, they can be taught to hone their perceptions, search for a unique approach, and try to bring clear thinking to clear writing. Students become better writers as soon as they find you are going to read their work, correct it, criticize it, and make them responsible for writing it, rewriting, and reading it to the class. They immediately begin to think about what they are writing instead of just writing. The same is true with style.

When you begin pushing for the unique, the unusual, the off-beat, the thoughtful, the perceptive, they will try to find if it is in themselves. All your students will improve, and a few will actually develop a style.

Scope: The purpose of this activity is to make clear that style does not replace substance. A discussion on the difference between fashion and fad helps clarify this point. The activity involves a class discussion and in-class writing or homework.

Process: Discuss with students the concept of fad versus style. For a more mature audience the discussion might be: Has there ever been a period when a woman was not smartly dressed in a black dress? Has a man's grey pin-striped suit ever left the fashion scene? *Classics.* That is what good writing is—timeless. For a younger audience the question might be: Do you buy two pairs of knock-off Nike's at a shoe discount store or the real thing at a well known and established department store?

After this discussion you may want students to revise some of the previous writing activities asking the students to more strongly focus on creating their own style, their own voice.

ACTIVITY 58: RECOGNIZING STYLE IN WRITING

*T*he tendency for most students at this point is to overwrite. Too often I read articles in magazines where the author is more dominant than the subject. That is overwriting. Students usually do it with too many adjectives and adverbs as a means of creating style. When you begin editing students' work you will get them to move from "All of a sudden Mark was exhausted" to "Suddenly Mark was exhausted," to "Sweat ran down Mark's face blinding him to the reality that he could go no further." (Ever notice in students' work that everything happens "suddenly"?)

Scope: This activity helps students to recognize quality of writing, style, when they hear it. It involves students listening to some writing samples and then discussing the most effective sentences.

Process: Read to students samples A and B and then ask them to choose the best writing.

A: Behind him walked his opposite, a huge man, shapeless of face, with large pale eyes, with wide sloping shoulders; and he walked heavily, dragging his feet a little, the way a bear drags his paws.

B: In reverse order came his antithesis. A gargantuan individual with nondistinctive facial features and extremely large pale tinted eyes, with a breadth of shoulders that traversed to the right; and his languid motion created drug feet the way a tainted marsupial locomotions at night.

A: If growing up is painful for the Southern Black girl, being aware of her displacement is the rust on the razor that threatens the throat.

B: Existence in the politically and socially unjust South is arduous, but being cognizant of not having ties to ancestral roots is even more devastating.

A: It was Sunday. Chance was in the garden. He moved slowly, dragging the green hose from one path to the next, carefully watching the flow of water. Very gently he let the stream touch every plant, every flower, every branch of the garden.

B: Sunday morning was optimal time for Chance to irrigate the various forms of floral in the garden. With great diligence he gave each plant the required portion of water. Equally as reverent the flow of aquae nourishment reached each flower and tree appendage.

Perhaps I have overdone the examples, but students tend to think ten-dollar words are superior to short, strong nouns and verbs in simple declarative sentences. Steinbeck's *Of Mice and Men*, Maya Angelou's *I Know Why the Caged Bird Sings*, and Jerzy Kosinski's *Being There* are not improved merely by turning to *The Guide to Expensive Synonyms*.

ACTIVITY 59: INTRODUCING TONE

Scope: *T*his activity introduces students to the subtle variations of tone in writing. It involves oral presentations and discussion and should take about half the period.

Process: Explain to students that tone is the author's attitude toward the subject. How does the author feel about apartheid, flowers, a fishing trip, the making of the Constitution? While journalists try to tell you they only report the facts, why is it that the same facts can be reported so differently? For example:

A: President Bush spent only $449 million on aid to the handicapped last year.

B: President Bush spent well over $440 million on aid to the handicapped last year.

Ask students if these authors were trying to make a point in reporting "just the facts"? Explain that even so-called unbiased journalists show tone.

   Next, tell students that a writer should be recognized in the first few words of the piece. Read the following examples and then ask students to describe the author's attitude, based upon tone.

Mary is one of the thousands of unfortunate girls who have become victims of cocaine.

Mary is one of the thousands of girls who took the easy way out and snuffed out their lives rather than face their hardships.

Both tones are conveyed by the selection of a few significant words. When we read fiction, reports, or op-ed writing, we want to feel the author's passions.

   Have students listen to the following example and compare it to the previous two.

Mary Lincoln, 17, of Hillhaven High School, was the 3,001st person in New York City to die of a cocaine overdose.

Good for a newspaper filler, but not an essay.

ACTIVITY 60: PRACTICING VARIOUS TONES

Scope: This activity further trains the students' ears to recognize and effectively evaluate tone in writings. The activity involves some reading to students and oral writing. It takes about half the period.

Materials: You will need samples of three authors' work with greatly varying tone. Any Poe, Salinger's *The Catcher in the Rye,* and some dialogue from Hemingway provide good contrast.

Process: Read a few lines of any three authors with varying tone in order to convey to students how tone is projected by how authors choose words. Have students label each of the readings with a single tone word, such as *dark, sarcastic,* or *macho.*

ACTIVITY 61: REVISING FOR TONE

Scope: This activity further develops the students' sense of tone and ability to choose the right words to create the right image. It involves students listening to sentences, modeling on the board, and in-class writing. It takes most of the period.

Process: Read to students the following sentence and, if they aren't laughing, ask them to explain why the word selection doesn't seem to work.

The raging river cascaded over the jagged rocks tumulting drift wood against the bank. Bambi loved this watering hole.

Read the second example and discuss.

Delicately he lifted her face towards his and reverently brushed a single strand of golden hair from her full, red mouth. He longed for her and then snapped her neck like a toothpick, the twit that she was.

Explain that tone must be consistent; how words are placed together creates tone. "Raging river" has a much different tone than "ambling brook."

Provide students with a noun and ask them to put a word in front or in back that fits. Then have them put one in front or back that doesn't fit. For example:

tattered antique
glitzy antique

neon dullness
effervescent neon

Do as many examples as needed for students to grasp the concept.

ACTIVITY 62: INTRODUCING SHOW, DON'T TELL

*A*nother important aspect of developing style and creating an effective tone is to show, not tell the reader. A major weakness of students' work is their reliance upon telling the reader the conclusions rather than giving the reader the information and letting him/her arrive at the conclusion. The reader wants to experience what the author experienced, not be told it.

"Show, don't tell" is my most common comment on students work. It indicates immature writing. The writer doesn't know how to convey the story, thus merely summarizes, complete with conclusions.

Scope: The purpose of this activity is to introduce the concept of showing, not telling, when writing an essay. It involves oral rewriting as well as in-class writing or homework. It takes two class periods.

Process: Read the following sentence to students and ask them to identify it as a show sentence or a tell sentence and explain their choice.

My grandmother is very perky for her age.

Read aloud the sentence below. Again have students identify it as a show or tell sentence and why. Have them determine which sentence is more effective and why.

Grandma Sonja has just bought her third Corvette, broken up with her second boyfriend in six months, and continues to follow the Grateful Dead from city to city.

Give the class these typical tell, rather than show, sentences and have them orally revise them to show.

This is a really interesting movie.
I had the best time at Great America Amusement Park.
Football is the best sport.

The first attempts at revision may be the same sentence with a *because* added. "This is a really interesting movie because it has lots of special effects." That is still telling, just more specific. Have students try again with these next examples. You may want to do these in written form either in class or at home and then have students share their results. Explain to student that perhaps they should rethink the concept and not the sentence in order to create a sentence that shows rather than tells.

Going to Vietnam was very, very hard on soldiers.
No one should take drugs.
My mom is the best.

You may want to share these revisions with the students.

Greg sits in the dark a lot. He jumps at loud noises. He has been addicted to drugs for the past 15 years. He is a Vietnam veteran.

In 1988, 300,000 more cases of drug addiction were reported in this country. The death rate for first time users is up 22 percent. The 15-year-old girl in a cell for having robbed an old man to get money for cocaine is not interested in these facts, only in getting her drugs.

It wasn't the first time Mom had saved me. She is always there when I need her. Sometimes it is my forgotten gym clothes, once some personal dance lessons. And the money I borrowed from her must be in the thousands by now.

Explain to students that the fewer conclusions you give your readers the better. You do need to present the reader with enough information to come to the desired conclusion. Point out to students that this single correction in writing approach will render their work fifty percent better immediately.

ACTIVITY 63: IDENTIFYING DIFFERENT POINTS OF VIEW

*T*he final element of writing techniques and an aspect of style, is development and consistency of point of view. On a basic level, point of view refers to maintaining the same tense throughout a piece of writing. This needs to be stressed with students. Additionally, point of view refers to who is telling the story. Not only does this need to be clearly established in the beginning of the work, it must be consistent throughout the work.

Scope: This activity forces students to work on writing from varying points of view on the same subject. It involves a short set of directions and writing homework.

Process: Students are to take a simple experience: brushing teeth, taking a test, sleeping, fixing a bike. They are to write the essay about the experience from their own point of view and then another short essay from the point of view of the inanimate object: the teeth, test paper, bed, bike, or whatever.

ACTIVITY 64: NURSERY RHYMES AND POINT OF VIEW

Scope: *T*his activity will help students focus on the concept of point of view by dealing with writing with which they are very familiar. It involves a short set of directions and either in-class writing or homework.

Process: Explain to students that most nursery rhymes are written from the third person, past tense point of view. Ask students to choose a nursery rhyme, fairy tale, or Mother Goose story and revise it from first-person-character point of view. Share and discuss these short works.

ACTIVITY 65: POINT OF VIEW AND FRAME OF REFERENCE

*S*imilar to point of view is what social scientist writers call frame of reference. As Henry A. Giroux explained in his address to the National Council of English Teachers:

"Frame of reference appears to be another complex but essential concept for students to understand. . . . Frame of reference can be defined as a general set of moral, social, and political beliefs and attitudes that forms an individual's way of both seeing the world and regarding a particular subject. A frame of reference is what disposes a writer to shape information in a specific way, to use a particular organizing idea."

Frequently when students are comparing topics for term papers, one student may abandon a topic because another student is writing about it. The student who concedes may feel that the definitive work is about to be written on the subject; thus there is no reason to also work in that area. Students need to be aware that a single topic offers unlimited frames of reference.

Scope: The purpose of this activity is to move students from the concept of point of view to frame of reference in order to help them select topics for essays. It involves discussion and brainstorming on the board. It may take most of the period.

Process: Explain to students the basic concept of frame of reference and how it is related to point of view.

 Have students pick an area (the Soviet attempt to unseat Gorbachev, for example), and brainstorm the different frames of reference that could be applied to that subject (for example, the role of the KGB; the role of the press; the psychological dealings between Gorbachev and Yeltsin; how the public was kept informed; how historians will evaluate the impact of this event). Too often, students feel that a paper is always merely a chronology of recounted events. Try this brainstorming exercise with your students on a number of topics.

• *Revision* •

Revision is the most difficult step of the writing process to teach to students. It is hard, it is often boring, and it means throwing away something of themselves. Convincing students that all writers do it and it is a necessary step to effective communication is the first goal. First, revision is not a handwriting exercise—it is a thinking activity. The first draft is the skeleton, the successive drafts apply the flesh, the look, the personality. This is a good time to review the synonyms for revision that Theodore Cheney gives. (See page 9.)

 Using lots of prewriting activities helps show students how to do revision. The prewriting activities are designed to help students with a final draft, they are not the draft itself. Thus, students begin to see revision is restructuring and rethinking, rather than copying over.

 Revision is like a treasure hunt. You know what you are looking for, sort of. By searching your mind, other writings, your proceeding words, the thesaurus, you find the treasure: the right word. It is an exhilarating process when you realize you have found the approach, the phrase, the word that communicates exactly what you had in mind.

Three words that my students are reminded of almost daily in writing class are: BREVITY, CLARITY, SPECIFICITY. These are the three goals of a final draft.

In the following section, activities are presented to individually examine clarity, brevity and specificity. Finally, a few brief activities teach all three goals.

ACTIVITY 66: INTRODUCING BREVITY THROUGH WANT ADS

Scope: *T*his activity will give students practice in writing with brevity. The activity involves a brief set of directions and writing in class and sharing. It can take an entire period.

Process: Have students write want ads for a new principal/teacher. Remind them that each word costs money. They must also remember that what they advertise for is what they'll get.

Have students share their want ads and discuss how brevity could be further achieved in some of the ads.

Ask students to write want ads for a new brother/sister/mom/dad, for some object for their bedroom, or for a new world. Emphasize that brevity should not be pursued to the point of lack of clarity. Read the ads aloud. Evaluate which ads work and why.

ACTIVITY 67: REVISING FOR BREVITY

*W*illiam Strunk explains: "Vigorous writing is concise. A sentence should contain no unnecessary words, a paragraph no unnecessary sentences, for the same reason that a drawing should have no unnecessary lines and a machine no unnecessary parts. This requires not that the writer makes all his sentences short, or that he avoid all detail and treat his subjects only in outline, but that every word tell."

Scope: This activity will give students practice in writing with brevity. The activity involves oral revision and in-class writing. It will take one class period.

Process: Ask students to revise the sentences below, paying particular attention to the use of the active-positive voice. Students should strive for brief, clear, specific language.

This has been a very, very rainy and wet April Showers month. (It has been a wet April.)

Owing to the fact that he had not completed the six units of college course work, his request for renewal of his about-to-expire teaching credential in education was denied. (His request for renewal of his teaching credential was denied because he had not completed six units of course work.)

We need a four-day extension on the subpoena so that James St. Claire, President Nixon's attorney, can evaluate and make judgment in terms of a response. (This sentence was written by Ron Ziegler, former press secretary to President Nixon. It shows that some sentences are so confusing they can't be rewritten.)

Have students work on these sentences:

Lance is one who cannot remember things very well.

Helping my mother has always been very enjoyable to me.

This being the month of July, one could say we have an abundance of moisture.

I have found it to be true that, as I look out through the window, it does, indeed, appear to be very dark outside at this time.

To practice writing with brevity further, ask students to revise the sentences on Worksheet 20. It is important for the revisions to be shared in class so that students realize that brevity can be achieved a number of different ways.

Get students to realize that revision is not just crossing out a few words. Often it is totally restructuring the sentence and approaching the point in another way.

Have students develop their own sentences that suffer from lack of brevity and revise each other's work.

ACTIVITY 68: ORAL BREVITY

Scope: The purpose of this final activity on practicing writing for brevity has the added feature of introducing speech to the class. The goal is still to work on brevity—getting the most information presented clearly in the least amount of space. The activity involves a short set of directions and either in-class writing or homework.

Process: Ask students to choose a famous person, living or dead. They are then to choose a situation such as an awards show, an airport welcome, a banquet, or whatever, where they are to introduce this famous person. They only have 30 seconds of speaking time. Explain to students they must focus on a strong lead, presenting the relevant informational background and providing a strong punch conclusion all in 30 seconds. Have each student present the speech in front of the class.

ACTIVITY 69: PRACTICING CLARITY THROUGH NURSERY RHYMES

"But that's what I meant." My standard response is, "But that is not what you wrote." Most students' work suffers from lack of clarity merely because they are not taking the audience into consideration. It is typical that students write for the teacher, rather than for a specific audience that does not have background information on the topic. When students accept the goal of communicating effectively, they will begin to be concerned about clarity. Keep asking them, "What does this writing say? What does it mean?"

Scope: This activity will introduce the concept of clarity and allow students the opportunity to focus on this skill through oral and in-class writing. It will take most of the period.

Process: Explain to students the first step to clarity is choosing the perfect noun and verb. Have students choose a simple nursery rhyme "Mary Had a Little Lamb" and revise it, changing all nouns and verbs. (You may want to introduce the thesaurus as part of this activity.) The main intent of this activity is to work on clarity, but developing more specific images is also a goal.

Students love sharing this assignment.

ACTIVITY 70: FINDING NEW CLARITY

Scope: This activity provides students an opportunity to practice writing for clarity by working on choosing the ideal nouns and verbs.

Process: Have students choose a paragraph that they have written and underline all nouns and verbs. Have them look up each noun and verb in a thesaurus to see if there is a clearer word.

ACTIVITY 71: BUMPER STICKERS MUST BE CLEAR

Scope: This activity continues teaching students the importance of clarity, especially when using only a few words. It involves brainstorming and in-class writing. It can be completed in one period.

Materials: Felt tip pens and paper the size and shape of bumper stickers.

Process: Have students brainstorm bumper sticker messages. After listing these messages on the board, discuss with students why authors were able to convey a clear message in so short a space. (Students often want to expand the discussion to personalized license plates.)

Have students write their own bumper stickers. The first attempts are usually variations on someone else's message, but have them keep trying. When some good ones have been written, pass out felt tip pens and the paper and have students create original bumper stickers. Display the bumper stickers and discuss. The focus of the discussion should be on how effective clarity of message is achieved.

ACTIVITY 72: EDITING FOR CLARITY

Scope: This activity forces students to edit their work with an eye to clarity, brevity and specificity. It involves a short set of directions and either in-class writing, oral writing, or homework. All work effectively. It will take an entire period.

Materials: Photocopied sheet of the worst sentences taken from the students' past work. Having students submit their own choices for worst sentences is a good option.

Process: Pass out the sheet of bad sentences and ask students to revise them. Have students discuss their editing choices and evaluate which choices create more clarity, brevity and specificity.

ACTIVITY 73: WRITING RIGHT

Clarity can only be achieved using sound technical skills. Teaching these boring rules can make even a teacher nod off in mid-sentence. Like practicing your golf swing wrong in order to understand how to correct it, learning the rules of clarity through breaking them is also effective—and a lot more fun.

Scope: Learning how to edit for clarity, brevity, and specificity by recognizing the inaccuracy of some improperly written writing rules is the goal of this activity.

This activity can be done as an oral class activity, in groups, or as homework. It provides a multitude of options. It is important to share the students revisions and thus identify the real purpose of the activity. The activity will take an entire period or more.

Process: Give students Worksheet 21; have them find the errors in the writing rules. Students should correct a rule or write why the rule is inaccurate. Not all rules can be corrected in the same way. Have students share their revisions.

ACTIVITY 74: WRITING WHAT YOU MEAN

Scope: This activity continues to engage students in revising for clarity, specificity and brevity. It is best done as a discussion with in-class writing so that students can discuss and debate their revision choices. It takes an entire period.

Process: Pass out Worksheet 22 and ask students to revise the sentences. Discuss with students their choices and which choices are most effective.

ACTIVITY 75: INTRODUCING SPECIFICITY THROUGH CONNOTATION AND DENOTATION

Scope: While student writing is often technically correct and clear enough, it often lacks the specifics that create strong communicative prose.

How many essays have you read beginning with "The book . . ."? Immediately you write in the margin, "What book?" It is difficult to set up isolated activities to teach specificity, but learning how specific language influences how the message is received does help teach the lesson.

This activity will take two to three class periods. It involves oral presentation, modeling, in-class writing, and homework.

Process: Define and discuss with students the words *connotation* and *denotation.*

Explain to students how to determine the connotation and denotation of a word by walking them through the following as you write it on the board.

> **World Series denotations:** *A series of seven baseball games played between the winner of the National League and the winner of the American League. First team to win four games is world champion.*

> **Connotations:**

Sight	Sound	Taste
banners	crack of bat	hot dogs
green fields	pop of ball in mitt	peanuts
red clay	national anthem	soft drinks
foam on beer	cheering	dust
uniforms	booing	

Smell	Touch	Feel
cut grass	smooth ball	cheering
nachos	splintery bat	anxious for victory
pine tar	embossed ticket	panic over call
		pride
		longing to play

Students are to create a chart similar to the one above for their word or phrase.

Once they have completed the chart, go on with the next step. Explain that connotation can be created using nouns, verbs, and modifiers. For example:

war:
blood, power, helicopters (nouns);
stupid, glorious, loud, stark (modifiers);
kill, bomb, bleed, shoot, steal, destroy, save (verbs).

Explain that connotation touches all of the senses: screams, smoke, dry mouth, blood, cold bayonet, scared.

Show how connotations can be both negative and positive.

For example:

fire:
provides warmth on a cold day; can destroy a home and kill people.

rain:
washes out the river and floods the city; provides needed moisture for the crops.

When students have understood the concept, have them choose a word and fill out Worksheet 23.

Students should then take the worksheet and use it as an outline for an essay. A second assignment could be to write the essay again but change the connotation and point of view. Each time the goal is to work toward specificity.

ACTIVITY 76: CREATING SPECIFICITY THROUGH THE INTERVIEW

*T*his activity can be used as a pre-writing activity when teaching interviewing, if you prefer to use it there. However, the activity does help emphasize the importance of specifics in writing.

Scope: The purpose of this activity is to use the interviewing technique to give students a sense of the need for specificity when writing. It involves some class discussion led by the teacher, some in-class pre-writing activities and homework. It will take at least two class periods.

Process: Have students choose a fictitious person such as Goldilocks, Cinderella, Superman, Smurfs, Miss Piggy, Bart Simpson, or whoever. They are to assume they have interviewed this character and are writing a story for *People* magazine. The focus of this activity is not on humor or fantasy, but on coming as close as possible to a typical, interview style magazine article. It may not be a Q–A (question and answer) style write-up. The article must stay in character at all times and provide the kind of specificity that readers want.

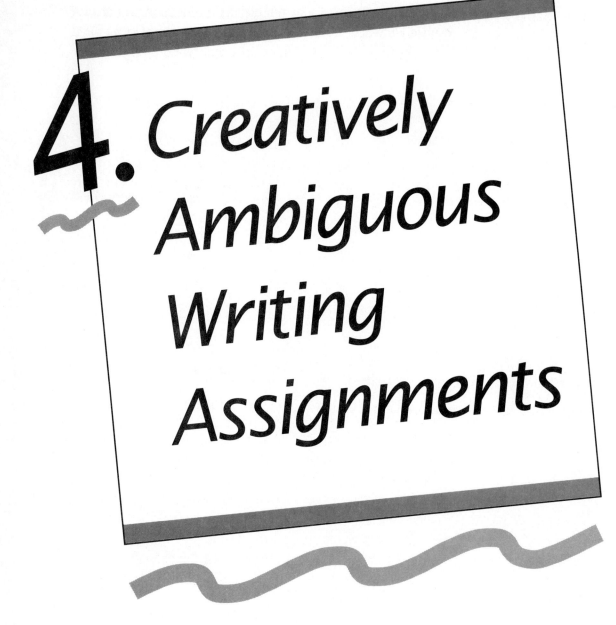

4. Creatively Ambiguous Writing Assignments

*A*t this point the students should have a solid grounding in the elements of writing. While the early sections focused primarily on teaching skills and learning process, this unit is essentially a series of writing assignments stressing the three major goals of writing, using creatively ambiguous kinds of topics.

There is no necessary order to these assignments. While the earlier sections followed a logical sequence, this chapter simply presents assignments that you may find helpful in eliciting quality responses from your students.

Most of these activities are designed for a paragraph or very short paper of half to three-quarters of a page. It should go without saying that whenever possible allow students to share their writing.

ACTIVITY 77: FOUR SEASONS

Materials: *R*ecording of Vivaldi's "The Four Seasons"

Process: Ask students to divide a sheet of paper into four sections and to label the sections "Winter," "Spring," "Summer," and "Fall." As you play short sections of Vivaldi's "The Four Seasons," have students use their senses to record impressions in these columns.

At the conclusion of the listening, ask students to develop a short essay which compares the four seasons (or how Vivaldi saw the four seasons) or to write an essay on one season which conveys the force and meaning of that season. The music, not their well-worn images of the seasons, should provide the stimulus.

ACTIVITY 78: ZODIAC SIGNS

Materials: *H*oroscope readings from the daily newspaper and a common astrology guide book.

Process: Read some of the signs as students identify their own. Then read some information from a basic astrology book. Each student will write an astrological interpretation of one of the twelve signs of the zodiac.

Students will fill out Worksheet 24 as a means of preparing to write. When the students have completed the worksheet, they should then write a profile of the personality for people born under this sign. Students may want to deal with what these people are like as children, how parents should deal with them, what their general behavior and characteristics are, what signs they do and do not mix with well, what types of careers these people generally gravitate towards, what they should watch for during the month ahead, and so on. The objective is not humor but to duplicate the style and format of astrology and horoscope writing. Choose the best ones, label them with dates, and publish an astrology guide for the school. Attaching teachers' names to each of the "months" will make the guide even more interesting.

ACTIVITY 79: EXCUSE ESSAY

"*M*y dog ate it." This excuse has been used so much it has now become a cliché. Surely your students can create much more exciting, plausible, outlandish, creative excuses.

Process: Ask students to write an essay on why their homework is not completed. Sharing these essays orally is always great fun. I'll always remember the time one student took out a pile of ashes and said she would like to read her paper, but a dragon had set it on fire, and this was all that was left.

ACTIVITY 80: NURSERY RHYMES, FAIRY TALES, AND MYTHS

Process: *H*ave students take a nursery rhyme, fairy tale, myth, or any children's story and write a modern version or develop a new character. See Appendix C for one fifth-grader's finished product.

Share with students what some of the psychological interpretations of these stories could be. They should then choose one and do their own psychological version to share with the class.

ACTIVITY 81: ORIGINS OF LIFE

Materials: *B*ooks on the origins of life from the Greek, Native American, African, and other cultures.

Process: Read some of the stories about the origin of the universe and life. Have students develop their own myths to explain the origin of life. Focus on clear explanation of the unexplainable while still hooking the reader.

ACTIVITY 82: BACK TO THE FUTURE

Process: *H*ave students brainstorm and cite some of the world's most important and far reaching events. Once a significant list has been developed, have students assume that they are the editor of *The New York Times,* and that everything that has ever happened, happened last night: What would be their ten front page stories in order of importance for tomorrow's edition?

Have students choose one event that they feel they would like to change. Have them develop an essay on why and how they would change it and what the results would be if they did change it. How would the world be different, better or perhaps worse if they did succeed in changing the course of history? Students must be as plausible in a nonplausible situation as they possibly can.

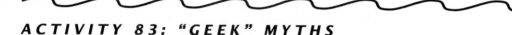

ACTIVITY 83: "GEEK" MYTHS

Materials: Copies of Greek and Roman myths which explain natural phenomena.

Process: After reading these myths, students can create some of their own characters and myths to explain everyday occurrences. For example "Socataures—the monster that lives in the dryer and steals one sock," or "Zitroneous—the god that is jealous if anyone is in love and causes a gigantic pimple just before an important date."

ACTIVITY 84: RULES FOR LIFE

Materials: Kim Williams was a hometown colleague and a long time favorite on PBS radio with her rural wit and wisdom. Get a copy of her book *(Uncommon Sense)* and share some of her lists for living.

Process: Have students brainstorm some of life's major problems: how to cure a broken heart, how to get a date to the prom, how to make the football team, how to cure pimples, how to live with a little brother, how to survive your mother's divorce, and other tribulations of everyday life.

Have students write a brief introduction defining the problem and give their own list of ten rules for living with or solving this problem. They should explain how the rules will work. Compile these lists and introductions into a guide for living.

ACTIVITY 85: LISTS, LISTS, LISTS

A technique to take roll requires students to write lists. Writing is writing—it doesn't matter whether it is a note, an essay, a paper or just a list, it is still making decisions about which words to choose.

Process: You should have a set of topics, but also allow students to choose the topic for the day. *The Book of Lists* volumes by Irving Wallace and others are good sources for ideas. "Subjects I Want to Study," "My Favorite Places," "Four Tasks I Want to Accomplish," "My Five Best Traits," "Ten Cities I Want to Visit," "Ten Items in My Room," "Seven Ways I Waste Time," "Five Ways to Say Something Positive," "Five Colleges I'd Like to Attend," "Six Possible Careers for Me," and so on all provide thinking and writing opportunities.

ACTIVITY 86: WRITING ON MORAL DILEMMAS

Materials: *C*hess board and pieces; knowledge of Shakespeare's "Measure for Measure" or a recording of Hal Holbrook's "Mark Twain Tonight."

Process: Bring in a chess board to class and set up a bind situation (no matter what white does, black is going to take a piece).

Next discuss either the moral dilemma in Shakespeare's "Measure for Measure" where Isabella must decide whether to sleep with Angelo in order to save her brother Claudio; or from Hal Holbrook's "Mark Twain Tonight" the selection "Huck's Dilemma" in which Huck must decide whether to identify Jim as a slave or not. (Other similar situations of moral dilemmas will also work.) Ask students to write on one of the following topics or on a similar topic that fits the particular unit you are studying.

Ask students: What was Huck's moral dilemma? What are the binds in "Measure for Measure?" Is there anything which you would not sacrifice in order to save your brother (sister, mother, father)? Have you ever been in a situation where both choices were bad? What did you do and why?

ACTIVITY 87: THE FOUR ELEMENTS OF THE PERSONALITY

Process: The ancient Greeks believed the personality was made of four elements: earth, air, fire, water. Discuss this concept with the class.

Have students brainstorm words that they associate with each of the four elements. Have students determine the percentage of each of these elements in their personality. Pair up students and have them estimate the percentages for their partner and have them share the information. Students usually want to do you or to have you guess them.

Once students have a clear grasp of the symbolic significance of the four elements, they are then to write an essay explaining their personality in terms of the elements (and what percent of each) they choose for themselves.

ACTIVITY 88: IMPOVERISHED PROVERBS

Materials: *Dictionary of American Proverbs*, ed. David Kin, Philosophical Library: New York, 1955.

Process: After reading some of the proverbs to the students, have students combine part of one proverb with part of another. For example:

An apple a day gathers no moss.
A bird in the hand saves nine.
Early to bed laughs last.

Have students offer a rational, logical explanation for this irrational bit of advice.

ACTIVITY 89: FRACTURED FABLES

Materials: *A* book of fables.

Process: Read some of the short fables to the class and discuss the genre in terms of form: e.g., basically a short story, generally about two animal characters that have human traits, in which a lesson called a moral is learned.

Have students do some brainstorming about possible lessons to be learned: for example, all people deserve to be treated fairly; trying to change yourself for others is wrong; honesty is the cornerstone of friendship—other student generated ideas.

Students should now choose their two animals and the traits of each. Once these decisions are made, they can begin deciding on a plot for their fable. The focus of the assignment should be on appropriately duplicating the fable format and on presenting the moral.

ACTIVITY 90: WORDS: ORIGINS AND CONFUSABILITY

*H*erbert Kohl's *Insight* has a wonderful section on words, their origin and their confusing nature. Words might seem to be a dull topic. It isn't. Kohl uses this section primarily as a creative way to teach spelling, but it is a great source of topics for essays. Some books that Kohl suggests for teachers can be used as research material for students. These include Room's *Dictionary of Confusibles,* (fiend, friend, find; assure, insure, ensure; abdicate, abrogate, arrogate, derogate).

Another great source is *Who's What,* which gives the background on Achilles' heel, Mrs. O'Leary's cow, and other such items.

Did you know that "disaster" means "against the stars?" This kind of information is found in *Therein Hangs a Tale.*

A discussion of such clustered phrases as heartfelt, hearty, heartless, heart-to-heart talk, heart warming, eat one's heart out, occurs in *A Dictionary of American Idioms.*

Two recent volumes that I have found fascinating are *Cultural Literacy* and *Encyclopedia of Things That Never Were.*

If your first inclination is to look at these books as resources for Trivial Pursuit, you are missing their real value. They present a wealth of information on why our language is as it is. For example, having taught *Lord of the Flies* a number of times and had wonderful speculative discussions on the nature of the title, I read yesterday in *Encyclopedia of Things That Never Were* that Lord of the Flies is an old name for Satan.

Process: Share these research books with your students, and then get creatively ambiguous and assign some topics for essays. The research and writing possibilities using these sources are endless.

ACTIVITY 91: IF ALL ELSE FAILS, ESSAY TOPICS

Process: Assign students topics from the following list of possible essay assignments adapted from Herbert Kohl's *Insight: the Substance and Rewards of Teaching* and from topics in my college entrance essay class.

From Kohl:

Having Power Over Adults

Running Away From Home

Finding Someone to Express Your Innermost Thoughts and Feelings To

Feeling Rejected.

Overcoming Some Weakness or Handicap

Having Secret Powers.

Being Poor or Homeless

Fairness/Unfairness

Why I Am Not Allowed To (Eat, Wear, Sleep) When I Want

I never, never, never passed out a list of possible topics and let kids choose one and write an essay—until this summer in a writing seminar. The topics proved successful so I share them with you. Don't just pass out the list, incorporate them into your learning plan.

Discuss your most embarrassing situation.

Discuss your thoughts on death.

What would it be like to fly?

What would you see if you rode through space on a beam of light?

If you were to have a dinner party and could invite four famous people, living or dead, who would they be and why?

Describe a weird or disgusting habit you have.

Explain how something functions—but don't use the correct explanation.

Explain why something that is false is really true.

Explain the difference between a white lie, red lie, and a yellow lie.

If your house was burning what would be the one item you'd save and why?

Explain sound to a deaf person or color to a blind person.

Choose one word that describes you and explain why that is the best word.

5. Putting It All Together: Major Papers

*T*he earlier writing activities were presented in a logical, sequential order in which writing skills were taught through the processes of prewriting, writing and revision. The assignments emphasized short written work. The strategies in this section are broader in scope. They require long term research and writing. The initial activities teach some methods in prewriting that can be adapted to any major paper or term project. These assignments are followed by some specific long range work and the section ends with some open-ended methods for developing term papers.

I do not recommend assigning activities in this section without having grounded students in the elements of writing through the activities in the preceeding sections.

• *A Sense of Purpose* •

ACTIVITY 92: WRITING THE PURPOSE STATEMENT

*O*nce students have learned to cluster and outline, the next step should be to learn to write a purpose statement. This three-to-five sentence paragraph tells the reader the precise purpose of the paper.

The primary value of the purpose statement is to have students focus themselves, more so than focusing the reader. Lots of time spent on the purpose statement will result in less time pondering what should go into the final draft of the work.

Process: Have students begin with a brief review of the informational lead. Next, give students two or three topics and ask them to write purpose statements as if they were going to write a major paper on the subject. Be sure that they consider what they will not include, as well as what they will include in the paper.

Review these orally. Keep in mind the question: Does it help focus the scope of the paper's topic of presentation?

Assign a purpose statement; require approval before allowing students to proceed with any research or writing on a major paper.

• *Developing a Position* •

ACTIVITY 93: THE POSITION PAPER

*S*imilar to the purpose statement is the position paper. This technique is used primarily for controversial topics but adapts itself to many other assignments.

Materials: Articles on controversial subjects from newspapers and magazines.

Process: Clip controversial paragraphs from newspaper and magazine editorials. Check various newspapers so that you can gather clippings on both sides of each question.

Give a pro-side clipping to half the class and a con-side clipping to the other half. Students are to write one sentence that identifies the issue. What exactly is the problem or conflict? Make sure they do not write how they feel or what their position is; they should define and identify the issue.

Get both the pro and con sides to agree on the language for a definition of the issue. For example, in a murder case the issue might be defined as

Did John Doe kill Mary Berra with a knife on January 22?

Once the issue has been defined, students are to prepare a rebuttal paragraph to the article originally given them. Students are to address themselves to only the points in the articles. Pro and Con groups then switch clippings and repeat the process.

Finally, each student should write a three-sentence paragraph in which the issue is defined, the position on the issue is clarified, and a piece of evidence is offered to support the position.

ACTIVITY 94: IDENTIFYING THE ELEMENTS OF THE POSITION PAPER

Process: *O*nce the process of developing a position statement has been learned, pass out Worksheet 25 that presents the elements of a controversial position paper and ask students to fill it out using complete sentences. This worksheet can be incorporated into a larger assignment or serve as an outline for development of a major paper.

Modification of this basic format can be used in many ways. The idea is to get students to commit to writing exactly what the topic or issue is and what their position is, and to determine what kind of information they will need to build a case for that position. The categories can be chosen as the situation warrants. What is important is that students are forced to put in writing what they are thinking and researching about the topic, and where they are and are not going with their paper. A road map is essential to any trip.

ACTIVITY 95: POSITIONS VIA CRITIQUES AND REVIEWS

*M*uch of the writing done for school comes close to being reviews of research at best and regurgitation of other's writing at worst. Often, term papers are critiques and evaluations of others' works.

Materials: Newspaper and magazine reviews.

Process: Read some examples of movie, concert, play, ballet, or book reviews. Assign students to go to a movie, play, concert, ballet, restaurant, or read a book, listen to a record, watch a television documentary.

Assign them to do some research and find out what others have said about their topic. *Book Review Digest,* newspaper and magazine entertainment sections, Sunday supplements in major newspapers, television shows, newscasts can all provide a quotation to be incorporated into the paper.

Ask students to write a review of what they saw or heard. Remind them that they are writing as critics for a newspaper or magazine and not as students of the class. The quotation should be incorporated into their paper.

In discussing the final papers, point out which students presented their own opinions with supporting evidence and which merely presented a revision of the researched material.

ACTIVITY 96: DEVELOPING A POSITION INTO AN ESSAY, A PERSONAL OPINION PIECE, AND A LETTER-TO-THE-EDITOR

Materials: Editorials from newspapers and magazines.

Process: Have students cut out an editorial or column from a newspaper or magazine. In no more than 200 words, they are to state the writer's position and why that particular position is held.

Next, have students write, in no more than 400 words, their position on the same theme and why they hold it.

Finally, have them write a letter to the editor expressing their views, using only 50 words. The point is to get them to work on developing their own position by clearly defining the issue, considering the alternative positions, choosing and weighing evidence, and then clearly and concisely presenting their position.

This type of activity is invaluable when dealing with research material and attempting to produce an original paper.

• *Utilizing the Packet Format* •

One method of making long term writing projects manageable is to develop a series of mini writing assignments into a packet. Students can handle a series of smaller writing assignments much more easily than three or four pages of directions on writing a major paper. The following packets cover autobiographies in a new way, a novella, an issue-oriented assignment, career education, and a journalism style project.

ACTIVITY 97: AUTOBIOGRAPHY PACKET

*M*any teachers have assigned an autobiographical essay and been disappointed with the results. The topic is much too large for students to handle well. This packet is a series of 15 assignments designed to give form to development of an autobiographical work. Rather than just saying, "Write about yourself," these prewriting assignments help a student to create "chapters" in their autobiography.

Scope: This activity will take a couple of weeks to complete. It will involve class discussions, modeling, out-of-school research, writing in class, and homework.

Process: First discuss with the class the difference between biographies and autobiographies. Discuss the motivations authors have when writing their autobiographies. Lead them into a discussion of the value of record keeping and how the phone has ruined any chance for a collection of great letters ever to be collected again. Talk about Alex Haley's *Roots* and how it spurred an interest in genealogy. Develop enthusiasm for personal and family investigation. Explain how the final product would make a wonderful gift to the family. Each of the following assignments should be given one at a time. Don't assign the whole packet at once; it would be a bit overwhelming.

Name Essay: Students are to write an essay about their name which would include some of the following information: What is the formal and informal version of your name; who were you named after; does the middle name have significance; who named you; what would your name have been if you were the other sex; what does the name mean; what is the language/ethnic background of your name; what is your name in other languages; do you like your name; if not, what name would you like; do you have pet or nicknames; do you have names picked out for your children?

Personal Situation Essay: Using the following phrases, have students brainstorm some personal situations:

Excitement over an accomplishment . . .
Anticipation of . . .
Anxiety over . . .
Disappointment . . .
Anger because . . .
Most embarrassed when . . .
Proudest when . . .
My biggest fear was (is) . . .
My greatest desire is . . .

Students then use these to develop an essay which describes the situation, what they did about it, and the outcome. Students may include a number of these situations in their book.

Time Line: Though not really an essay, it is a writing assignment. Discuss time lines and show some examples from typical historical research materials. Have students write a family time line or just one for their own life. The time line should be complete with pictures.

Heraldry: Introduce students to the concept and historical significance of heraldry. Show them examples of coat-of-arms. Have students develop a personal coat-of-arms and write an essay explaining why they chose the elements they did. If they have a family coat-of-arms they may want to show both and compare them.

Genealogy Interview: Discuss and show examples of family trees and have students develop their own. Students should then contact the oldest member of their family tree and conduct an interview with them. An account of the process and what they learned in reconstructing the family tree also makes for an interesting essay. Have students pay particular attention to famous groups of people or ethnic groups to which they are related.

Personal Recipes: Discuss the two parts of a recipe: the ingredients and the process. (See Activity 21.) Have students pair up and write in recipe form directions for duplicating the other. The focus isn't on humor, but on capturing the essence of the personality and characteristics of the partner.

Family Scripts: In most families there is an identifiable "party line." It is the sense of family place, expectations, values that have been handed down from one generation to another. "We Grahams always do our best." "The Donovans have always produced doctors." "It is the nature of Murphys to volunteer." "The Reads have never been afraid of hard work." "The Youngs have always exhibited an artistic flair." Have students see if they can identify their family "line." What is the kind of motto your family lives by? Have students develop an essay explaining this motto and how they are working to live up to it.

Quotations to Live By: Have students examine *Bartlett's Famous Quotations* and other quotation anthologies to find a quote they feel expresses their values, their goals, their way of life, their philosophy. Students then write the quote and an essay explaining its meaning and how it applies to how they want to live their life.

Birthday: Have students research what famous people were born on the same month and day they were. Have students review newspapers of the day and year they were born. They should review some of the major events of the year they were born. Have students gather this material and discuss the significance of that date.

Personal Narrative: Discuss and read examples of the idea of first-person narrative writing. Have students write a first-person narrative essay about a real event in their life that led to an understanding or realization on their part.

Character Sketch: Discuss and read examples of character sketches. Then have students write a character sketch of the most interesting person in their family. They should look for material beyond the physical and focus on the emotional and mental characteristics of the family member.

The Future: Have students prepare a specific essay which examines what they feel their life will be like from now until they are 30 years old. What will they be doing? How will they have gotten there? Where will they be living? What about a family? Are they happy? Why/why not?

Documents: Have students ask family, relatives, coaches, teachers, religious figures, friends, or whoever knows them to submit statements for inclusion in their autobiography (a letter of recommendation, for example). Have students then gather documents for their book, copies of birth certificates, school report cards, airline tickets, passports, confirmation, awards, newspaper clippings or whatever.

Personality: Have students find a magazine picture (not of a person) that best illustrates their personality. Have them write an essay about why the picture represents them. Display both picture and essay in the book.

Finally, have students gather all of this material together in some creative manner and present it to the family as their autobiography. It will be a major document for the family.

ACTIVITY 98: THE NOVELLA/SCREENPLAY PACKET

Scope: This activity will take one day of orientation and a number of days of either in-class or out-of-class writing.

Materials: Ten slips of paper about 1" by 4" for each student and eight containers for the slips.

Process: Pass out ten small slips of paper to each student. What they write on these slips should be kept confidential.

First have students write a specific place (for example: Paris, France, a small cafe near the left bank). All students should place these slips in the container marked "Setting."

Next have students list four objects on a separate sheet (for example: a pack of gum, a map, a Swiss army knife and a rose). These slips would go in the container marked "Props."

On two slips of paper, students are to write two brief character descriptions (for example: Boris, 32, Russian, walks with limp; Jeanette, 21, ballerina, French, beautiful). These should go in the container marked "Characters."

Now students should write an international diplomatic secret (for example: The Red Chinese have developed a weapon that disintegrates uranium without harmful side effects). This slip would go in the container marked "Secret."

Next have students write a character sketch for an ally (for example: Beanie, 17, computer whiz, has asthma). This slip should go in the container marked "Ally."

Now students write their special power or skill (for example: forgery). These slips should go in the container marked "Powers."

Then students write their fear (for example: snakes). These slips go in the container marked "Fears."

Finally, students identify a second place thousands of miles from the first one (for example: Calcutta, India—the home of trade merchant Iraji Brundee). These slips go in the container marked "Objective."

Pass Worksheet 26 to students. Have students draw slips for one category at a time. Repeat the process until students have chosen slips for all categories and completed the worksheet.

The students' assignment is to write a suspense thriller. The paper will be judged on how cleverly they incorporate this seemingly unrelated material together into a coherent story that utilizes all the elements given them. These are great fun to share.

ACTIVITY 99: CREATING THE COMMERCIAL PACKET

Scope: This activity will involve discussion in class, group working time, writing, and art work creation.

Materials: The film "60 Seconds," reel-to-reel records or cassette recorders with two decks, and various art materials.

Process: Show students the film "60 Seconds" about the making of a 7-Up commercial. Or engage in a discussion of some of the more effective and least effective commercials. Vance Packard's *The Hidden Persuaders* is well worth examining.

First, divide students into working groups. They are to write a proposal on the product or service they want to sell, the audience they want to sell to, and the image they are going to attempt to create for their product or service.

Then students are to prepare list of positives and negatives about their product or service and write a short essay on how they are going to accentuate the positives and ignore or down play the negatives.

Next, students must write a script for a radio commercial.

Using reel-to-reel or two deck cassette tape recorders, sound effect records, musical instruments, junk, records, tapes, and anything else, students are to create a 60-second radio commercial complete with copy and sound effects. Students are to focus on creating an effect, an image, as well as an argument to persuade the listener to buy the real or imaginary product.

When the commercial is complete, they are to write a letter to their employer explaining the scope of their radio commercial and to the company making the product explaining why it will like how they have portrayed the product.

Have students play their commercials for each other and write single paragraph critiques.

As a final activity, have students write an ad that discourages people from buying the product or service. The focus should be not on humor but on accuracy. For example: Did you know Brand X's cheeseburgers supply you with four times the recommended amount of daily salt?

ACTIVITY 100: FROM MUSIC SCORE TO SCREENPLAY

*M*ost student writing cannot sustain a theme or plot line for longer than a chapter or two. The purpose of this packet is to help students stay focused and not write themselves out in the first chapter. It encourages students to learn that a story is developed, not spontaneously written.

The method I chose to teach this sense of long term development based upon a well thought out plan was to approach a movie in reverse. Give the students the music score first, and then write the movie to fit the score.

I was overwhelmed with the impact of the movie *The Mission*—both its sound and visual beauty. I bought the tape and chose five short sections of music with a recurring theme but with a change in tone and color. This became the sound score for the students' future novella or screenplay written in prose form. It is important to remember that a music score is not written for every word of the movie or every second of film. It occurs, fades out, recurs— sometimes for a few seconds, sometimes for a full song. Thus the music is merely the inspiration, the tone setter for the story.

Scope: This activity will involve in-class listening to music, discussion, and writing, in addition to homework writing. It takes about one week to complete.

Materials: Make five short tapes of music which have a recurring theme but a change in tone and color. Real movie scores are a good source, but make sure the movie is not current. Don't share the movie title with the students.

Process: Give students Worksheet 27 and ask them to complete it as directed.

Step 1: Key Words. Have students listen to the five tapes and as they do, have them write key words that come to mind as inspired by the music.

Step 2: Window on Literature. Once they have listened to the tapes at least twice and finished Step 1, have them decide on the setting, characters, plot line, and theme of their screenplay. These notes should be brief and to the point. They are just beginning to focus their story, but they should be thinking about the total, not just the first few paragraphs.

Step 3: Plot Points. The following class period, play the taped music segments one at a time and have students fill out Step 3 in the worksheet according to your directions.

Chapter 1: Introduce setting, characters and basic plot line— set up the story. List the basic idea of Chapter 1.

Plot Point 1: This is a major occurrence that sends the story in a new direction that is plausible. It moves the story forward. What is the event?

Chapter 2: Development of plot line, depth of characters exposed, theme clarified. List the basic idea of Chapter 2.

Chapter 3: Confrontation/Conflict Setup: Is it human against nature, against self, against another human. The theme and the plot line are united by this point. What is basic setup of Chapter 3?

Plot Point 2 (a major occurrence as in Plot Point 1):

Chapter 4: Determination of Resolve established. The events must be in order so that the ending in the final chapter is plausible and holds together. What is basic plot line of this chapter?

Chapter 5: Resolution. The story concludes for reader and the plot line.

Step 4: Questions. The next day, play the tapes again and have students answer the questions as they listen.

Step 5: Write/Revise/Present. Once students have filled out Worksheet 27 they are ready to write. You should be constantly reading their worksheets and questioning them. Does the story hold together; is there consistency; is the story manageable; do students have a feel for theme and plot line; does the story reflect the music or is it just a story rather than being an interpretation of the music score?

Each day play one chapter tape; have students write a chapter for the next five writing classes. They can replay the tapes as often as they want. After Chapter 3 has been written then start the process of peer and teacher editing and commenting. By this time it is too late for copying.

This technique has been used with fourth graders through adults and is most successful. You will find that no two stories are the same. When students are done with a final revision, have them pass their stories around so they can read as many as possible. Publish them.

This same kind of technique could be used with a single piece of music and the worksheets could be adapted to your particular curriculum needs.

ACTIVITY 101: THE ISSUE ESSAY PACKET

Scope: The packet approach is applied to an essay on a current issue.

Process: Brainstorm with the class current issues such as Soviet reorganization, abortion, drugs, cheating in schools, pollution, sex education, the United Nations' role in Persian Gulf War, terrorism.

Next pass out Worksheet 28 to students. Have them complete the steps one at a time in order. When the packet is complete, they are ready to write a major paper on a current issue.

This prewriting packet approach is probably one of the most valuable techniques I have developed for teaching students to focus their writing. Forcing them to commit to where their writing is headed is invaluable for getting where they want to go. This form can be adapted and modified to fit any curriculum need.

ACTIVITY 102: THE CAREER ESSAY PACKET

Scope: *T*he packet approach is here applied to a study of career possibilities. This three-page packet is developed by the student over a long period of time. Research begins to be stressed as a preparation for writing.

Process: Brainstorm with students a list of possible careers. Once an extensive list has been generated, pass out Worksheet 29 and have students complete it.

ACTIVITY 103: INTERVIEW PACKET

*A*s a writer for *People* magazine I was always amazed at how easy it was to get an interview with someone who traditionally denies interviews, if you had the right approach. One of the best approaches is being a student journalist. Famous people generally like contact with young people and think that students can't hurt them in print. A student can often get an interview that a professional journalist cannot. This packet is designed to help students get the important interview. Later, perhaps, you can help them sell the piece.

Process: Have students complete Worksheet 30 as they did the previous packets. The process is what creates a quality product in the end.

I have found that students who follow this plan faithfully will often not get an interview with a star, but will get a good interview with the agent, the personal secretary, someone else in the band, another actor on the show, the senator's aide, or whatever. Have students do an interview with someone as close to their subject as possible.

There are a number of good books on conducting journalism style interviews. Pick one appropriate for your grade level. Bring in a local journalist to give a workshop on interviewing.

STAMINA OVER THE LONG HAUL: MAJOR PAPERS

*H*aving completed assignments in each of the previous sections of the book—which teach skills, focus thinking, develop research abilities—students should now be ready for major research and writing assignments.

The four activities in this section are slightly less traditional approaches to what is generally referred to as the term paper. The object of these activities is to provide a format for students to work on lengthy research and writing assignments and develop the skills for maintaining writing stamina on larger projects.

ACTIVITY 104: TERM PAPER OF ELEMENTS

*T*o do any writing, students must first be able to tell you what it is they want to write about and from what focus. If students tell you Russia is the topic they have chosen to write a paper on, find out what they really mean before allowing them to continue. Do they really want to write a paper on Soviet-American relations? If so, during what period and on what specific issue? Students need to learn to focus their papers.

Scope: This activity will involve class discussion, peer editing, conferencing, research, and in- and out-of-class writing. The length of the activity will be determined by how extensive you want to make the assignment.

Process: Brainstorm with students possible topics for their paper and have them move from a one-word explanation of a topic to a five-word, ten-word, single-sentence, and then single-paragraph explanation.

Pass out to students Worksheet 31 and discuss each step with the class. Students should then begin to complete each step, with class time used for conferencing, peer editing, and sharing of problems and written material.

This procedure will ensure that adequate time is being spent on each item and that the students are progressing in a logical manner. By evaluating each step of the process before students go on to the next step, you have a built-in quality-control method.

Next, students should write a purpose paper that will give the topic focus. As explained in the purpose statement assignment, (Activity 92), this paper should be one page on exactly what the students are going to write about. Are they going to analyze, compare, contrast, identify, reconstruct, question, chronicle, or what? Use of these focusing words is critical. Students should make it clear, by using the words, what they are attempting to accomplish.

Students should then write on what they already know, believe, feel, or suspect about their topic. This, too, should be done in a page or less.

A researcher must have some idea what information is needed in order to write a paper. Therefore, students should take what they already know about a topic and develop a list of questions to be answered while doing research.

Then have students hand in a detailed bibliography of possible sources. If you approve the sources, students should begin investigating the research materials. Information that appears to be helpful should be written on index cards, with a full citation of the sources at the bottom of the card. (Standard footnote and bibliography forms can be found in grammar-composition textbooks.)

Once students have done the research that time allows, have them go back and reread the research cards, giving each card a subject heading at the top left-hand corner. From these subject headings, students should write an outline to be handed in for evaluation. The research cards should then be ordered according to major category. Then the cards within the category should be arranged in a logical order.

After the reordering of the cards, an extensive outline should be written and cards abandoned that do not fit the paper's plan. Students should now write a one-to-three page introduction. The more time spent here, the less time will be spent organizing the text of the paper. A well-constructed developmental introduction will carry an average paper.

When the introduction is finished, students should determine whether it needs to be refocused.

Next, they should complete the conclusion.

Then they should reread and revise.

Finally, students should check the paper for technical errors (verb tenses, subject-verb agreement, spelling, capitalization, punctuation).

ACTIVITY 105: RESEARCH PAPER

Scope: *T*his approach lends itself to historiography or literature-analysis papers. The purpose of such an assignment is to read and analyze extensive amounts of information on one subject, question, author, or period. This activity will involve in-class writing, homework, discussion, peer editing, conferencing, research. How long the activity takes is determined by how extensive you wish to make the assignment.

Process: After students have gone through the topic selection process described earlier, they should develop a bibliography. The bibliography must be broad-based and include all sides of an issue. Once you have approved the bibliography, students begin reading the books and other works in the bibliography. Not all of the work needs to be read; students may only need to read certain sections or chapters. As the students do their reading they take notes. The first note for a selection should include a full citation for reference: full name of author, exact title, publisher, date of publication, place of publication, edition, number of pages in book, specific number of pages read for the note. Following the citation is a summary of a certain number of pages. For example:

From David Gar, The Agrarian Crusade. *Belmont, CA: Hickey Press, 1947, 222 pages: pp. 19–82: After war, crop acreage and production increased, prices dropped, farmers in a state of depression. Great panic of 1873 lasted throughout decade, hit farmers especially, many lost farms through foreclosures, blamed monopolies and railroads. Railroads welcomed by farmers at first, later condemned because of watered stock, land grants, high freight rates. Farmers had 7% of representation in Congress, 47% of population engaged in agriculture.*

Students would then consider factors that influenced the author's views, such as class, economic position, political affiliation, education, family. Much of this information can be found in any good contemporary author resource book, such as *Contemporary Authors.*

The students should then make a brief statement as to whether the work is based on original source material, secondary sources, or both.

Next, students should state the author's purpose: Was it written as a doctoral thesis, to vindicate the author's point of view, under a grant from an organization or a fellowship from a think tank, to make money, or what? Students should cite the biases that dominate or influence the book, as well as point out the main themes and conclusions in this work.

Finally, students should critique the book: Was it worthwhile? Based upon the research, the student should develop an essay question specifically geared to the findings. This is then answered in a 5–8 page essay. The question should challenge the student to use the research to create a quality answer. This forces the student to go beyond regurgitation of researched material.

ACTIVITY 106: NON-TERM PAPER PAPER

Process:　　　　　*H*ave students choose some subject they want to investigate. Once they have done the research, they should decide on the medium for presenting the information. They can, for example, do a slide show with accompanying narration, a super 8mm film, a video tape, a cassette-tape presentation, a radio program of interviews and narration on reel-to-reel tape, a play, a photo album, an art display, or any multi-media combination. The point is that for this assignment, a paper cannot be the mode of transmitting the research.

Have students brainstorm the many possible modes of sharing information. Once they have conducted some of the research, they should develop a plan of communication.

• *Alternative Writing Curriculum* •

Bernard Percy, in his useful volume *The Power of Creative Writing,* offers writing teachers an entire writing curriculum without even knowing it. It is contained in his glossary. As I read his glossary it came to me that merely talking about each one of these words each day and then assigning students to write samples would be a terrific curriculum guide. I have adapted his definitions. Not all his words are used. Words that were already emphasized in early activities are eliminated, as are words that do not relate to the basic focus of this book. If you like the definition approach to writing, here is a useful set of writing terms.

ACTIVITY 107: MODES OF EXPRESSION

Process:

*E*ach day explain one of the terms below and discuss some examples. Then have students write their own example.

Allegory—A story with an underlying meaning, different from the obvious, surface, or apparent meaning. It can be read, or written, at different levels: 1) reacting to the surface story; 2) looking for the theme being communicated by the story; 3) deciding who or what the story characters, places, or events represent in the real world.

Allusion—An indirect reference to something, using a metaphor.

Analogy—A comparison of things, showing a similarity between things that are unlike in other ways—for example, comparing a computer to the human brain.

Anecdote—A short narrative of an interesting incident or event.

Antithesis—The placing of two sharply contrasting ideas in adjoining sentences or next to each other in one sentence: "Give me liberty or give me death"; "To err is human; to forgive, divine."

Aphorism—A concise statement that expresses a general thought or truth: "A bird in the hand is worth two in the bush."

Autonomasia—Using the name of a person, usually well-known, as a substitute for the name of another person having similar characteristics: Instead of saying "Here comes Pete," say "Here comes Don Juan."

Cadence—The rhythmic flow or pattern of words in poetry or prose.

Deduction—Going from the general to specifics; presenting the conclusion first (the point to be proved), then giving the evidence that supports that conclusion. (The reverse approach would be induction.)

Euphemism—A mild or indirect term or expression instead of one that is harsh or unpleasantly direct. "Sanitary engineer" is a euphemism for "garbage man."

Expository essay—This essay clearly explains or conveys facts and ideas.

Idiom—A phrase or expression whose meaning cannot be understood from the usual meanings of the words: "Kick the bucket"; "I am under the weather."

Irony—An expression that says the opposite of what is really intended: "Hey, fatty" said to a very skinny person; "It sure is beautiful," during a miserable streak of weather.

Maxim—A statement of general truth; a short rule of conduct: "Think before you act," "Look before you leap."

Parody—A humorous imitation of a serious piece of writing, using the style of that piece.

Portmanteau word—A word formed by putting together parts of other words; these words convey an effect and show meaning by echoing one or more familiar words: "smog" from "smoke" and "fog."

Satire—A poem, essay , story that ridicules or holds up to scorn people, habits, customs, and ideas.

Synecdoche—A figure of speech in which a part is used for the whole. "Count heads" for "count people."

Worksheets

• *Overview Evaluation* •

Name_____ Class_____ Date _____

Author of paper evaluated:_____

Assignment:_____

Either orally or in writing, answer the following questions after having read your partner's essay.

1. For fifteen seconds tell very quickly what are the main points, main feelings, and the major focus of the essay. Say what comes to mind. For example: "It was bright. I felt the warmth of the beach. Lots of color. The drowning was sure a shock. Felt sad." _____

   _____

   _____

   _____

   _____

2. Summarize it into a single sentence. _____

   _____

   _____

3. Choose one word from the writing which best summarizes the work.

   _____

4. Finally choose a word that isn't in the writing to summarize it.

   _____

• *Self-Evaluation* •

Name_____ Class_____ Date_____

Assignment:_____

_____

Purpose of Paper:_____

_____

_____

Strongest Points Made in Paper:_____

_____

_____

_____

_____

Weakest Points in Paper: _____

_____

_____

_____

_____

Technical Errors: (Give page/paragraph/line)

spelling:_____

tense: _____

usage: _____

capitalization: _____

punctuation: _____

lack of clarity: _____

• *Peer Evaluation* •

Name_____ Class_____ Date _____

Author of paper evaluated:_____

Assignment: _____

Answer yes or no to the following questions:

1. Paper has title:_____

2. Paper has strong lead: _____

3. Paper has an introduction paragraph that sets focus and parameters: _____

   _____

4. Paper has a proper conclusion:_____

5. List page/paragraph/line of all technical errors: _____

   _____

   _____

   _____

6. List the main points you feel the author is trying to make: _____

   _____

   _____

   _____

7. List the strengths of the paper:_____

   _____

   _____

   _____

8. List those points you feel are weak, and explain why. List specific steps that could be taken to strengthen the paper: _____

_____

_____

_____

_____

_____

_____

_____

9. If you were doing the revision of this paper, on what would you focus your primary attention: _____

_____

_____

_____

_____

_____

• *Revision Checklist* •

Author:_____ Evaluator:_____ Date:_____

Paper Title:_____ Class:_____

Before beginning this evaluation, number all paragraphs in the student's essay. Respond to each item below; if it does not apply write DNA (does not apply). Remember to be helpful, not just critical. Be specific.

1. List those paragraphs by numbers that do not appear to have a topic

   sentence: _____

2. List those paragraphs that do not appear to have transition sentences:

   _____

   _____

3. List all those paragraphs where a quote, statistic, or example would

   strengthen the point the author is trying to make: _____

   _____

   _____

4. Give paragraph and sentence number of statements that you feel are unclear:

   _____

   _____

5. If you feel the progression of the paragraphs could be improved, list how you

   would reorder them. Make a list of those paragraphs you would eliminate:

   _____

   _____

6. List paragraph, sentence number and page with spelling errors: _____

_____

7. List page, paragraph, and sentence with punctuation errors: _____

_____

8. List page, paragraph, and sentence with capitalization errors:

_____

9. List page, paragraph, and sentence with usage errors: _____

_____

_____

10. List page, paragraph, and sentence with verb tense agreement errors:

_____

11. Write a paragraph that briefly explains the focus and major thesis of this
    paper. Assign it a grade. _____

_____

_____

_____

_____

_____

_____

_____

_____

_____

_____

_____

_____

• *Article Evaluation* •

Name_____ Class_____ Date_____

1. Bibliographic Notation of Article (author, title, magazine, date of issue, page
   it starts) _____

   _____

2. Major points author makes:_____

   _____

   _____

3. Means or techniques used by author to establish points: _____

   _____

   _____

4. Major points that are weak, and why:_____

   _____

   _____

5. Questions or points the author does not deal with that should have been
   discussed: _____

   _____

   _____

6. Your conclusions on author's presentation of this topic: _____

   _____

   _____

   _____

   _____

• *Nonfiction Book Evaluation* •

Name_____ Class_____ Date _____

1. Bibliographic notation (author, title, publisher, date published): _____

    _____

    _____

2. Author's brief biography:_____

    _____

    _____

3. Brief synopsis of book: (Focus, time frame, events) _____

    _____

    _____

    _____

    _____

4. Major points author makes:_____

    _____

    _____

    _____

5. Reasons and evidence author gives to support major points: _____

    _____

    _____

    _____

    _____

    _____

6. Evaluate style of author (consider clarity, smoothness, ease of reading):

_____

_____

_____

_____

_____

7. What are the strengths of this book?_____

_____

_____

_____

_____

8. What are the major weaknesses?_____

_____

_____

_____

_____

9. What have you learned from reading this book?_____

_____

_____

_____

_____

• *TV/Movie Evaluation* •

Name_____ Class_____ Date _____

1. TV program or movie title: _____

    _____

2. Brief synopsis of program/film:_____

    _____

    _____

3. What audience is the program/film attempting to reach?_____

    _____

4. What kind of message (theme) are the producers trying to present?_____

    _____

5. What means are used to present the message? (Be specific.) _____

    _____

    _____

6. How realistic is the program/film? _____

    _____

7. Evaluate the directing, acting, filming and writing. _____

    _____

    _____

8. What have you learned from watching this film? _____

    _____

    _____

• *What the Writer Does* •

As you listen to what Donald Murray says about writing, jot down ideas that occur to you.

1. The Writer Sees

2. The Writer Writes

3. The Writer Revises

• *Tools of the Writer* •

As you listen to what is said about writing, jot down ideas that occur to you.

1. Unity

2. Originality

3. Emphasis

4. Diction

5. Development

6. Conciseness

7. Coherence

8. Clarity

9. Audience

10. Active Voice

11. Sources

• *The Writing Process* •

Jot down ideas these headings suggest to you.

1. Motivation

2. Collecting Impressions

3. Rough Draft

4. Rereading

5. Sharing

6. Editing

7. Mechanics Check

8. Final Draft

9. Presenting

• *Situational Writing* •

Using the situations below, think about the situation in a unique way and write a single sentence inspired by that situation. DO NOT use what is written below as the first part of the sentence.

1. It is snowing.

2. You are lost in New York City.

3. Your mom is combing your hair.

4. You are underwater in Hawaii.

5. It is late at night and you hear your brother crying.

6. You see the morning sun come through your window.

7. You are alone.

8. It is Spring.

9. You are walking.

10. You reach into your pocket.

• *Geometric Writing* •

Make large copies of these figures on your paper.

Concept Brainstorm Circle

Cluster Circle

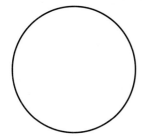

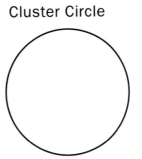

Parameters Rectangle

Support Blocks

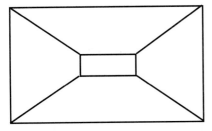

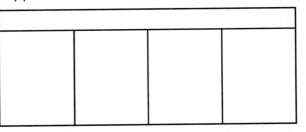

Style Rectangle

Focus Triangle

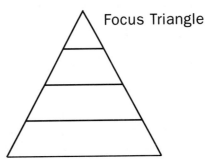

Draft Windows

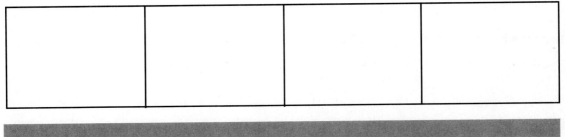

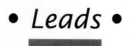

• *Leads* •

Thesis Restatement: (When given an essay question such as "What was the most important event in your life" the author would write . . .) The most important event in my life was being lost when I was 12 and figuring out what to do.

Informational: The purpose of this paper is to discuss the three major events leading to the entrance of England in World War 11.

Question: Can a panel of judges determine the most beautiful girl in America?

One Word: Violence. Today terrorism and riots threaten every traveler to the Middle East.

Quotation: "We will never negotiate out of fear and we will never fear to negotiate," stated President Kennedy in his Inaugural Address.

Flashback: As my younger brother graduated from high school, I remembered his first day in school.

Thrust: It was not the first time I had felt this panic. From the moment I entered the hall I felt my palms moisten, my heart beat rise and my brain seem empty. Taking the SAT's was going to be no different than the anxiety I had each Friday taking my spelling tests when I was in third grade.

Fact/Fiction: The tall grass of the plains gently stroked the roaming buffalo as Indians watched intently from the butte. This is the scene of Robert Benchley's popular novel *Only Earth and Sky Last Forever*.

Journalism: "To Build a Fire", written in 1902 by Jack London at his ranch in Glen Ellen, was the first modern short story to examine the relationship between human nature and politics.

Staccato: Breaking waves...salty air...matching sea and sky. This is the picture of Nice, France as one descends the Toulon Mountain toward the city.

© Addison-Wesley Publishing Company, Inc.

• *Leads Quiz 1* •

Identify each of the following leads by writing the style next to each lead.

_____1. Freedom. Three republics of Russia have chosen freedom by forming a commonwealth rather than stay members of the Soviet Union.

_____2. Ravaging press . . . upset women . . . legal battles. The William Smith trial elicited all of these.

_____3. Released hostages stated, "It has been more difficult than we expected, to learn to live with freedom again."

_____4. The fever pitch of the crowd indicated their disdain for the King, and they began storming the Bastille. This scene is eloquently portrayed in Charles Dickens' book *A Tale of Two Cities.*

_____5. Latvia, Estonia, and Lithuania today announced their independence from the Soviet Union in order to more fully achieve political independence.

_____6. The purpose of this paper is to evaluate the effectiveness of the NEXT computer in comparison with the Apple.

_____7. Can General Motors continue to use animals in car crash tests?

_____8. He turned another corner and could still hear the gang of teenagers behind him. Why had he chosen this route back to the freeway? The steps were getting louder and louder and the panic more intense. Gang violence in the city is beginning to touch more people than just gang members.

_____9. As I stepped before the jury to present my closing arguments, I had that same sense of preparedness as when I faced the college entrance committee.

• *Leads Quiz 2* •

Write a lead using the style and topic identified on this paper.

1. Staccato—a vacation trip

2. Question—a report on a current world problem

3. One word—a book you have read

4. Informational—a report on an artist

5. Thesis restatement—what you are most proud about yourself

6. Journalism—a school event

7. Quote—relations between the U.S. and South Africa

8. Fiction/Fact—report for history class

9. Flashback—holidays

10. Thrust—teenagers

• *Operative Words Test 1* •

Decide which operative word should have been used.

1. Tell how an apple and a feather are alike and different._____

2. What does love mean?_____

3. Tell me all about the functioning of a car. _____

4. Tell me why "Hook" is a great movie._____

5. Tell me about the beach this weekend. _____

6. Why did the Russian revolutionaries win in 1917? _____

7. Give me some examples of poverty in the world today._____

8. What happens when two hydrogen molecules are mixed with one of oxygen?

   _____

9. What are the main ideas from the *Time* article on death? _____

• *Operative Words Test 2* •

List the nine operative words and explain what you are supposed to do when given an assignment with that operative word.

1. _____

_____

2. _____

_____

3. _____

_____

4. _____

_____

5. _____

_____

6. _____

_____

7. _____

_____

8. _____

_____

9. _____

_____

• *Operative Words Test 3* •

The following assignments have operative words that were used inappropriately. In the blank, write what operative word should have been used.

1. Compare happiness._____

2. Evaluate the sights and sounds of a roller coaster ride._____

3. Describe which was the best movie of 1988._____

4. Define the main points of *Das Kapital.* _____

5. Contrast how Jack London's short stories influenced politics. _____

6. Discuss the working of a computer. _____

7. Define Japanese to Italian. _____

8. Prove a situation creating anxiety. _____

9. Illustrate that laser beams can travel in curved lines._____

• *Unity of an Essay* •

Jot down ideas that occur to you about each of the following.

1. Unity of Subject _____

   _____

   _____

2. Unity of Scope _____

   _____

   _____

3. Unity of Tone _____

   _____

   _____

4. Unity of Style _____

   _____

   _____

5. Unity of Point of View _____

   _____

   _____

6. Points on Tone and Emphasis _____

   _____

   _____

7. What Makes for Ineffective Tone and Emphasis _____

   _____

   _____

• *Revising for Brevity* •

Rewrite the following sentences.

1. Being that it is a particularly controversial subject involving a multitude of differing opinions both pro and con the newspaper advisor has chosen not to allow us on the staff to write any articles about this emotional subject.

2. By and far this is the most inspirational speech ever heard over the radio or in person by me since Father Paric spoke to our class last year at this same time.

3. My brother gave my sister an apple who has been sick in the hospital for three days, much longer than my brother was in the hospital last year.

4. Previously in the past it was the English Department's job to teach students at the school to write term papers, essays, stories, and other types of writing.

5. The idea is to involve the students in as many exercises as possible is the goal.

6. It seems to be the philosophy of most government officials to raise their pay annually.

7. How far up the ladder you can be promoted is entirely up to you there are no limits.

8. It may not be the most absolutely simplest way but it is often the best way unless you have your father do it.

• *Writing Right Rules* •

Find the errors in these rules. Then correct the rule or write why the rule is inaccurate.

1. Make sure each pronoun agrees with their antecedent.

2. Just between you and I, the case of pronouns is important.

3. Verbs has to agree in number with their subjects.

4. Don't use no double negatives.

5 Being bad grammar, a writer should not use dangling modifiers.

6. Join clauses good like a conjunction should.

7. A writer must not shift your point of view.

8. About sentence fragments.

9. Don't use run-on sentences you got to punctuate them.

10. In letters essays and reports use commas to separate items in series.

11. Don't use commas, which are not necessary.

12. Parenthetical words however should be enclosed in commas.

13. Its important to use apostrophes right in everybodys writing's.

14. Don't abbrev.

15. Check to see if you any words out.

16. In the case of a report, check to see that jargonwise, it's A-OK.

17. As far as incomplete constructions, they are wrong.

18. About repetition, the repetition of a word might be real effective repetition— take, for instance the repetition of Abraham Lincoln.

19. In my opinion, I think that an author when he is writing should definitely not get into the habit of making use of too many unnecessary words that he does not really need in order to put his message across.

20. Use parallel construction not only to be concise but also clarify.

21. It behooves us all to avoid archaic expressions.

22. Mixed metaphors are a pain in the neck and ought to be weeded out.

23. Consult the dictionary to avoid mispellings.

24. To ignorantly split an infinitive is a practice to religiously avoid.

25. Last but not least, lay off cliches.

• *Writing What You Mean* •

Revise these sentences to make the meaning clear.

1. People having relatives buried in this cemetery are requested to keep them in order._____

2. I shall wear no clothes as a means of creating individuality. _____
   _____

3. Those are good riding boots; they fit you and look well on a horse. _____
   _____

4. When the baby is done drinking it should be unscrewed and washed in hot water and left to dry in the dish rack. _____
   _____

5. Women are more likely to hit other cars and stationary objects than men.
   _____

6. Please excuse my daughter from class today, she had a fever so I had to have her shot. _____

7. The roses looked lovely coming down the garden path this morning._____
   _____

8. No one is allowed to sleep outside the camp but the guards. _____
   _____

9. She sat with her head in her hands and her eyes on the floor. _____
   _____

• *Connotation and Denotation* •

Word:_____

Denotation: _____

Connotation:

Sight	Sound	Taste	Smell	Touch	Feel
_____	_____	_____	_____	_____	_____
_____	_____	_____	_____	_____	_____
_____	_____	_____	_____	_____	_____
_____	_____	_____	_____	_____	_____
_____	_____	_____	_____	_____	_____

Positive Nature: _____

_____

Negative Nature: _____

_____

Nouns: _____

_____

Verbs:_____

_____

Modifiers: _____

_____

• *Horoscopes* •

1. New name for the sign of the zodiac: _____

2. Symbolic sign (hawk, volcano, flower): _____

3. Ruling planet (Mars): _____

4. Cosmic Color (red): _____

5. Lucky number (3): _____

6. Best feature of person born under this sign (eyes): _____

7. Best emotional feature of person born under this sign (courage): _____

   _____

8. Is this sign a fire, earth, water, or air sign? _____

9. Draw a symbol for this new sign.

• *Position Paper* •

Definition of Issue: _____

_____

_____

Position on Issue: _____

_____

_____

Argument in Favor of Position: _____

_____

_____

_____

Evidence to support argument: _____

_____

_____

_____

Anticipated Rebuttal to Position: _____

_____

_____

_____

Anticipated evidence to be used in argument: _____

_____

_____

_____

_____

• *Novella/Screenplay* •

You have awakened in _____.

You look around and see a backpack. You look inside and you find

_____, _____, _____,

and _____.

You are worried that the two spies chasing you, _____

and _____, will capture you and force you to tell

them the secret: _____

_____

_____.

You know the only person you can trust is _____.

You are hoping that your special power of _____

will help you overcome your fear of_____.

You have to get the secret to_____

where you'll meet your contact.

• *From Music to Screenplay* •

STEP 1. KEY WORDS

Chapter 1

Chapter 2

Chapter 3

Chapter 4

Chapter 5

STEP 2. WINDOW ON LITERATURE

Setting:	Characters:
Time:	
Place:	
Plot Line:	Theme:

STEP 3. PLOT POINTS

Chapter 1—the beginning, introduce setting, characters, and basic plot line—set-up of the story: List the basic idea of chapter 1.

Plot Point 1: This is a major occurrence that sends the story in a new direction that is plausible and moves the story forward. What is the event?

Chapter 2: Development of plot line, depth of characters exposed, theme clarified. List the basic idea of chapter 2.

Chapter 3: Confrontation/Conflict Set-up. Is it human against nature, against self, against another human? The theme and the plot line are united by this point. What is basic set-up of chapter 3?

Plot Point 2:

Chapter 4: Determination of Resolve established. The events must be in order so that the ending in the final chapter is plausible and holds together. Characters are enlightened or fall—theme prepared for resolve in this chapter. What is basic plot line of this chapter?

Chapter 5: Resolution. The story concludes for reader and the plot line.

STEP 4. QUESTIONS

1. What I want reader to feel at end of story: _____

   _____

2. What I want reader to learn from reading story: _____

   _____

   _____

3. How I want reader to respond from reading story: _____

   _____

   _____

4. Threads to my story: _____

   _____

   _____

   _____

5. What is the dramatic need of my main character? _____

   _____

   _____

6. What is the point of view of the story (for example, first person present tense)?

   _____

7. What is the feel? (dark, wet, foreboding?) of this screenplay? _____

   _____

8. Who tells the story? _____

9. What is the change that will occur in the story? _____

_____

_____

10. What is your attitude toward the subject? _____

_____

_____

11. In one sentence explain what the story is about. _____

_____

_____

12. In one paragraph explain what this story is about. _____

_____

_____

_____

_____

_____

13. In one sentence explain the realization/outcome of the story. _____

_____

_____

_____

• *Issue Essay* •

A. List the topic you have chosen for your paper. _____

B. In a single sentence write the purpose of your essay—use an operative word in your statement. _____

_____

_____

C. State the audience for this paper. _____

_____

D. List some resource materials you feel will be helpful in finding supportive evidence for your paper. _____

_____

_____

_____

E. Review this material and find at least three quotes that you can incorporate into your paper to support your position. List the quotations with proper footnote notation here:_____

_____

_____

_____

_____

_____

F. Outline or Cluster your paper on the back of this worksheet or on another sheet of paper.

G. Decide what method of development will best suit your essay and list it here.

_____

_____

H. Determine the tone or style your essay will have. _____

_____

I. Write a clear definition of the issue. _____

_____

_____

_____

J. Write a clear statement of your position on the issue. _____

_____

_____

K. Write your lead. _____

_____

L. Now write a brief outline of your paper in light of your new work. _____

_____

_____

_____

_____

_____

M. Having had each step of this packet checked by the teacher, go ahead and write your first draft.

• *Careers* •

1. List five career areas, not jobs. (science, sales) _____
   _____
   _____

2. List three specific jobs for each of the five areas. _____
   _____
   _____
   _____
   _____
   _____

3. Go through local papers and locate as many jobs as possible that are available in your areas of interest and attach them to the back of this worksheet.

4. List what you feel to be the best companies to work for at the jobs you are interested in having. _____
   _____
   _____

5. On another sheet of paper, write a letter to the Personnel Director of three of these companies seeking employment information and background on the company.

6. Do research on three of the jobs that are available—what training, education, experience required; path to the top; salary; locations of employment; skills need; number of jobs available.

7. Phone the Personnel Directors that you have written to see if you can visit the companies. If you can't visit, arrange to interview someone in the company.

8. On another sheet of paper, prepare 20 questions you intend to ask when you make your visit.

9. Write up a report concerning your visit and/or interview.

10. Write a thank you note to the company.

11. Write a debriefing paper about what you have learned about this career in general and this company in particular. Explain why (or why not) you are still interested in this field.

• *Interview* •

1. List 10 areas you are interested in. _____
   _____
   _____
   _____
   _____
   _____
   _____
   _____
   _____
   _____
   _____

2. List five famous people currently associated with each of these 10 areas. If you don't know any, research it. _____
   _____
   _____
   _____
   _____

3. Ask your parents, relatives and neighbors if they know anyone famous, or anyone they know who knows someone famous.

4. Choose three famous people you are going to work on simultaneously to get an interview. _____
   _____
   _____

5. List the possible professional organizations, unions, clubs, agencies, or companies that could help you contact these people. _____

_____

_____

_____

_____

_____

6. Write a focus idea for a story on each of these people. Each story must have a slant. A general background or a Q/A (Question/Answer) style article is dull. You have to think of a new approach. Lady Diane may want to give her views on child rearing. A star who has a mentally handicapped child may want to talk about that. A star who loves to cook may want to share recipes. A star who has an unusual hobby may want to address other hobbyists. Find the unusual slant if you want to get the interview.

7. Go through major city newspapers, Sunday supplements, magazines, entertainment journals, and watch television programs such as "Entertainment Tonight" to find out if these people are appearing anywhere so that you can contact them.

8. Go through *How to Contact Anyone Who Is Anyone* (by Michael Levine) and similar resource books and get a contact address. _____

_____

_____

9. Write a strategy for contacting them by phone and by letter. _____

_____

_____

_____

10. Prepare 20 good questions for each interviewee.

11. Put your plan in motion.

12. Decide your most likely interviewee and do background research on that one person. Begin to reevaluate your contact plan. Make sure you develop new questions based on your research. Don't ask questions that you can find the answer to yourself.

13. Keep track of all your contacts—names, phone numbers, comments.

14. Conduct the interview either by phone, by mailing a cassette and questions (or a typed set of questions), or in person. Write up the interview in the *People* magazine style. Or write an essay about the process you went through to get an interview and didn't get.

• *Term Paper of Elements* •

Below is a list of steps to be completed. Have each step completed and checked by your teacher before going on to the next step.

1. Focus statement—page or less

2. Preconception statement—page or less

3. Bibliography

4. 10–15 research cards (this is first phase of research)

5. Basic outline 1–2 pages

6. Additional research cards and ordering of cards

7. Extensive outline

8. Introduction 1–3 pages

9. Rough draft of main text

10. Revision of Introduction

11. Writing a concluding section

12. Reviewing and revising for technical errors

13. Final draft turned in

Appendix

• *Appendix A: Editorial Markings* •

Place period. ⊙

Add material here. ∧

Tie paragraphs together. no ⁋

Paragraph. ⁋

Lowercase. ℓar

Uppercase. rosa (underlined)

Delete. ℓ

Close up. ⌒

Misspelled. (mispell) sp

Comments refer to this material. [ ]

Unclear. unc?

Style. ( )

Ignore; correct. stet

Add space. #

Appendix B: Six Descriptions,
• Each Conveying a Different Impression •

In a wilderness cabin there is always a need to set or hang things outside. My canoe paddles go up under the extended roof, and there are hooks where I can hang a pot of stew to cool, out of reach of pets, sled dogs, or forest creatures. It is not unusual to come upon a cabin of this protective roof style and see snowshoes, packsacks, saddles, and other gear hanging up. These are the items that give a wilderness flavor to a cabin. Under such a roof, firewood can be stacked against the wall where it will be fully protected from the elements.

—Calvin Rutstrum
The Wilderness Cabin

Even the cabin was dismal and damp. I turned the gas mantle high, lit the kerosene lamp, and lighted two burners of my stove to drive loneliness away. The rain drummed on the metal roof. Nothing in my stock of foods looked edible. The darkness fell and the trees moved closer. Over the rain drums I seemed to hear voices, as though a crowd of people muttered and mumbled off-stage. Charley was restless. He didn't bark an alarm, but he growled and whined uneasily, which is very unlike him, and he didn't eat his supper and left his water dish untouched—and that by a dog who drinks his weight in water every day and needs to because of the outgo. I succumbed utterly to my desolation, made two peanut-butter sandwiches, and went to bed and wrote letters home, passing the loneliness around.

—John Steinbeck
Travels With Charlie

He was trying to farm stubborn ground and make a home in a cabin of logs he cut from timber nearby. The floor was packed-down dirt. One door, swung on leather hinges, let them in and out. One small window gave a lookout on the weather, the rain or snow, sun and trees, and the play of the rolling prairie and low hills. A stick-clay chimney carried the smoke up and away.

—Carl Sandberg
The Prairie Years

During the first week after moving into the cabin there was a lot of carpentry work to finish. Bunks had to be built of saplings set against the north wall, then covered with mattresses of sphagnum moss and caribou hides. Sleeping robes had to be made as well, and these consisted of deer hides placed with the fur side in, and sewed along three edges. Jamie built a table of flat rocks raised on stones to about two feet above the floor. Since there were no chairs, this was high enough. The boys crouched on two boulders, each of which had a cushion of caribou hides, and dined in style.

—Farley Mowat
Two Against the North

This was an airy and unplastered cabin, fit to entertain a traveling god, and where a goddess might trail her garments. The winds which passed over my dwelling were such as sweep over the ridges of the mountains, bearing the broken strains, or celestial parts only, of terrestrial music. The morning wind forever blows, the poem of creation is interrupted; but few are the ears that hear it. Olympus is but the outside of the earth everywhere.

—Henry David Thoreau
Walden

Serena Caudill heard a step outside and then the squeak of the cabin door and knew that John was coming in. She kept poking at the fireplace in which a hen was browning.

"Where's Boone?"

"Around, I reckon." She looked up then and saw him shut the door against the rain, saw him shut it behind him without turning while his eyes took in the murky kitchen. He limped to the wall, making an uneven thump on the puncheon floor, started to hang his coat on its peg, thought better of it and hunched it back around his neck. In the warmth of the room the smells of cow and sweat and drink and wet woolens flowed from him.

—A.B. Guthrie
The Big Sky

Appendix C:
• Alice and the Timekeeper •

The Timekeeper is an awkward, out-of-phase, clockman.

Generally, he looks like a clock with a face, two arms, and two legs. The numbers on his face are out of order. Clockwise, they read: 12, 7, 5, 1, 10, 2, 11, 9, 3, 6, 8, and 4. On his face are 4 hands sticking outwards from his nose. The shortest has small printing which reads 'century', 'year', and 'day'. All of these spin at various speeds.

As you can see, he is not an ordinary clock. If somebody asks a question, his answer will be the answer to the next question asked. This is because the time, in Wonderland, is backwards. So he remembers the next question asked, and answers it.

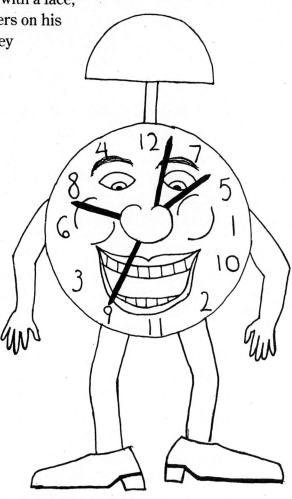

The timekeeper is a confusing clockman. He is always out-of-phase with other people's time.

As Alice walked down the path, she saw a big clock sitting off in the distance. When she got closer, she noticed it somewhat resembled a human. The human-clock stood up. Alice's pace lessened. Then she remarked to herself, "Don't be afraid, Alice! Why, it's just a little clock!" She finally stopped walking about 30 feet away from it. "How do you do, sir?" asked Alice. "Timekeeper", it replied. At this, Alice was confused and decided to try another question. "May I ask your name?" "Thank you", it said. Then Alice thought questions were useless and walked still closer. It was then she noticed the other features such as the 4 spinning hands marked 'century', 'decade', 'year', and 'day'. She also noticed the numbers on his face which were out of order. "You have an interesting face ", remarked Alice. "Good-bye!" it said in a cheerful tone. At this Alice was very offended. As she stomped down the path she repeated, "Good-bye!"

by Daryl Sisk, 5th Grade

Bibliography

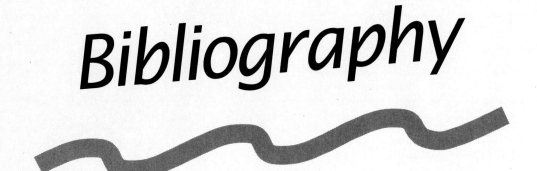

Atwell, Nancie, *In the Middle: Writing, Reading and Learning with Adolescents*. Portsmouth, N.H.: Boynton/Cook, 1982.

Beyer, Barry. *Teaching Thinking in Social Studies*, Columbus, Ohio: Charles E. Merrill Publishing Co., Inc., 1979.

Britton, James, et. al., *The Development of Writing Abilities*. London: Macmillan Education Press, 1975.

Cheney, Theodore, *Getting the Words Right: How to Revise, Edit, and Rewrite*. Cincinnati: Writer's Digest Books, 1983.

Cooper, Charles, ed., *Evaluating Writing*. Urbana, Ill: National Council of Teachers of English, 1977.

Cross, Donna Woolfolk, *Word Abuse*. New York: Coward, McCann & Geoghegan, Inc., 1979.

Dewey, John, *Experience and Education*. New York: Collier Books, 1938.

Elbow, Peter, *Writing Without Teachers*. New York: Oxford University Press, 1973, p. 86.

Elbow, Peter, and Pat Belonoff, *Showing and Responding*. New York: Random House, 1989.

Emig, Janet, *The Composing Process of Twelfth Grades*. Urbana, Ill: National Council of Teachers of English, 1971.

Fader, Daniel, *The New Hooked on Books*. New York: Berkley Publishing Co., 1976.

Flower, Linda S., and Elizabeth Haynes, "Problem Solving Strategies and the Writing Process," *College English*. December, 1977, p. 454.

Fraenkel, Jack, *Helping Students Think and Value*. Englewood Cliffs: Prentice-Hall, Inc., 1971.

Frank, Marge, *If You're Trying to Teach Kids How to Write, You've Gotta Have This Book!*. Nashville, TN: Incentive Publications, 1979.

Graves, Donald, *Writing: Teachers and Children at Work*. Portsmouth, NH: Heinemann, 1983.

Haynes, Elizabeth, "Using Research in Preparing to Teach Writing," *English Journal*. January, 1978, pp. 82–88.

Kalkstein, Paul. *Good Writing*. Belmont, CA: David S. Lake, 1982, Chapter 1, Sec. C.

Kellum, David, *The Socal Studies: Myths and Realities*. New York: Sheed & Ward, 1969.

Kohl, Herbert, *Insight: The Substance and Rewards of Teaching*. Menlo Park, CA: Addison-Wesley, 1982.

Miller, Casey, and Kate Swift, *The Handbook of Nonsexist Writing for Writers, Editors and Speakers*. New York: Lippincott & Crowell, 1980.

Murray, Donald. *A Writer Teaches Writing*. New York: Houghton Mifflin, 1984, pp 12–13.

National Assessment of Educational Progress, *Write/Rewrite: An Assessment of Revision Skills*. Denver: National Assessment of Educational Progress, 1977.

Newman, Edwin, *Strictly Speaking*. New York: Warner Communications, 1975.

Nostrand, A.D. Van, "The Inference Construct: A Model of the Writing Process," *ADE Bulletin*. May, 1958, pp. 13–30.

Percy, Bernard. *The Power of Creative Writing*. Glossary (Out-of-print but may be available in a library.)

Rico, Gabriele L., *Writing the Natural Way: Using Right-Brain Techniques to Release Your Expressive Powers*. Los Angeles: J. P. Tarcher, 1983.

Smuin, Stephen K., *Turn Ons!* Belmont, CA: David S. Lake, Publishers, 1978.

———. *Can't Anybody Here Write?* Missoula, MT: Mushroom Enterprises, 1981.

Strunk, William, and E.B. White, *Elements of Style*. New York: Macmillan Publishing Co., Inc., 1972.

Turabian, Kate, *A Manual for Writers of Term Papers, Theses, and Dissertations*. Chicago: The University of Chicago Press, 1967.

Wiener, Harvey, *Any Child Can Write*. New York: McGraw-Hill, 1978.

Young, Richard, Alton Becker, and Kenneth Pike, *Rhetoric: Discovery and Change*. New York: Harcourt Brace and World, Inc., 1970.

Zinsser, William, *On Writing Well,* San Fancisco: Harper and Row, Publishers, 1976.